ACCOUNTING

A Beginner's Guide to Understanding
Financial & Managerial Accounting

By John Kent

in this book.

By reading this document, the reader agrees that under no circumstances is the author responsible for any losses, direct or indirect, which are incurred as a result of the use of information contained within this document, including, but not limited to, — errors, omissions, or inaccuracies.

ACCOUNTING

Table of Contents

ACCOUNTING

INTRODUCTION

Accounting is one of those words that send shivers down the spine of even the most rugged individuals. When it comes to running a business, accounting is like the boogeyman that hides in the closet. It isn't that accounting is harmful, quite the opposite actually; accounting is a useful skill that should be part of your routine business. Many people start their businesses because of a passion, such as baking or carpentry. This passion fuels the desire to make a living through this manner and it is a delightful experience. Then accounting rears its head and the reality that running a business isn't simply fun and games sets in.

Accounting doesn't need to be this troublesome, though. There are numbers to be worked and this is intimidating to pretty much anyone who has ever sat through a high school math class. The truth is that accounting looks much harder than it actually is. It's one of those topics which becomes incredibly simple once you start to get your feet under you to form a solid understanding of how it is done. It still takes time and effort to ensure that you're not tossing away money through poor calculations, but this will come with time and there are accounting principles that are widely used and which help to make the process even easier.

With this book I aim to show you that accounting isn't as hard or as scary as you might have thought. We'll cover a lot of ground in a short amount of time but you'll be shocked at how little space you need for Accounting 101.

In chapter one, we are going to look at the importance of accounting. Why exactly is this skill so important? We're going to focus on accounting in businesses, rather than personal accounting. Some people will find that bringing this skill into their personal lives can improve their financial health but most people simply don't need it. However, we will briefly talk about tax accounting (and a few other types) in order to keep our eyes open to the ways we can continue to grow our accounting knowledge. Also important is the discussion we'll have on the difference between accounting and bookkeeping, two words which are often used interchangeably despite the fact that they aren't the same.

In chapter two we will lay down the basics of accounting. From the accounting equation to financial statements, we'll see what the main pieces of accounting are. This will be followed with a look at the principles of accounting in chapter three. These include acronyms like GAAP and IFRS, which seem far more complicated than they truly are when they're broken down into their letters this way. Once you shine some light on these, you'll realize that they're actually useful tools for making your life easier when it comes to your business's accounting process.

Chapter four will dive deep into financial statements. Get ready to learn all about the different statements you'll be using. These statements will help you to get a sense of where everything is and where everything is going, making sure that you have a clear and precise understanding of your financial situation. They really serve as the foundation for your financial decisions and you'll find that mastering them gives you a great advantage when planning what comes next for you and your company.

Chapter five will move into a discussion on the general ledger and how to proper record transactions. Without accurate accounting—i.e. updated and correct records—you can't make informed decisions. If you want to benefit from this skill set then you need to know how to record information effectively and without error. Again, this is an important process but one which is not nearly as difficult as you might think.

The last chapter will focus on managerial accounting. Managerial accounting deals with the internal aspects of the company. While financial reports and typical accounting must be done to a certain set of standards, managerial accounting stays inside the company and therefore it can use different metrics and standards to decide what is important. We'll look at how this form of accounting is used for goals such as forecasting and margin analysis.

By the time you finish this book, it is my hope that you will no longer see accounting as a monster in the closet but rather as one of the key tools at your disposal for ensuring that you spot financial problems before they are devastating. While it is always advisable to hire an accountant if you don't know what you're doing, it is important to take time and learn about these skills yourself. You may not want to take over your accounting duties yourself, even though it can be a way to save money, but a solid understanding will allow you to read and understand what you are being told so that you are never taken advantage of. To my mind, that alone is worth the price of admission for the book you hold in your hands.

CHAPTER ONE

IMPORTANCE OF ACCOUNTING

I can tell you that accounting is important but I'm sure that you've already heard this before. As soon as we start to look into launching our own business, no matter how small, we are buffeted with advice. Most of it simply stresses that you absolutely *have* to get an accountant. Or, depending on what part of the country you're in, you might hear "tax guy." Taxes are just another form of accounting and they typically mean it in a wider sense.

I am a firm believer that we don't follow advice in this manner. We can hear something a thousand times but never really get it. Instead of hearing what to do, it is important to hear why we do what we do. Once you understand the why behind accounting, all of the mystery dissipates and you see it in a new light. You might even see that it is easy to learn yourself if you're running a small enough business. The larger your business gets, the more the need for accounting increases, but so too does the size of the job. What takes a few hours for a smaller business takes up a lot more time once it's large. It is when accounting grows to this size that you are best served by hiring a professional for nothing else than letting you focus your attention on the problems that concern you the most.

In this chapter we're going to look at why accounting is so important for your business. With this grounding we'll then be able to look at the different forms of accounting there are such as financial, managerial, and tax accounting. There's other types too, but we'll cover those when we get there. We'll finish this chapter by clearing up an issue that confuses many people. Just what exactly is the difference between an accountant and a bookkeeper? Do you know? Or maybe they're the same thing? If you don't know the answer to these questions then don't worry, we'll sort all that out before heading on to chapter two.

Why is Accounting Important for Your Business?

There is a reason everyone has been telling you that you need an accountant. Accounting is one of the most important parts of keeping a business running. There are laws that have to be followed in regards to paperwork and money, otherwise you'll be running a criminal enterprise. That might sound a little bit extreme. I'm not saying you'll suddenly be part of the mafia or anything. However, your failure to follow regulations will lead to legal issues that will quickly shut down your business. If you don't run into this issue then chances are your lack of accounting led to financial issues that dropped the floor out from under your business.

The accountant's secret weapon is their ability to generate and analyse reports. Financial reports such as income statements, balance sheets, and cash flow statements all help to give you up-to-date financial information to understand exactly how well your business is doing. These statements cover things such as how much has been spent and how much has been earned by the company as a whole or over a set period of time. These might seem like simple documents and guess what? They are. But you're unlikely to use them until you understand how they are done and how to make the best use out of them.

As simple as accounting is when you first begin, you might think that keeping up on statements like these isn't very valuable. This tends to be an opinion that you see in much smaller businesses such as those with one to five employees, especially those that run online or don't require an office. These places have much lower overheads and so counting and following the numbers is much easier. The truth is that numbers, especially when it comes to finances, have a way of running away on us. It is just all too easy to overspend or lose track of where the numbers are supposed to be when you're keeping everything in your head. Study after study has shown us that we overvalue our memory's ability to retain information. By giving this information over to and running it through some basic accounting, you open your business up to a much greater range of tools and benefits.

One of the biggest benefits is that it reduces the chance that your business ends up on the wrong side of the law. Different states have different codes that must be followed in terms of what documentation you need to provide in order to run a legal business in the eyes of the IRS. There are tons of local laws that have to be followed about where you can open what business and what guidelines need to be followed for your industry and these may vary quite a bit, but you'll find that most states are closer together in terms of accounting regulations. You need to be aware of what liabilities you need to claim and, if you'll pardon the pun, be accountable for. These can be found with ease online for those looking to do their accounting themselves. An accountant for hire should be well-versed in local compliance already.

Beyond the legal side of things, it helps you to evaluate and operate your business from the most accurate perspective possible. By keeping accurate financial records you are able to manage your business much more effectively. Consider this on a small scale. You just work with your friend and you lend them the company credit card. When you get it back, they tell you they bought what was needed but forget to mention the can of pop they got. You're now working on slightly wrong information but if you jot it down and keep track then this can be sorted later. But what if you don't get back a price at all? Or what if you forget about that purchase on Thursday when it comes time to track everything next week? These are both arguments for why you need bookkeeping but this is going to have a direct impact on your accounting. In the short run you will find that your numbers are off and in turn this will cause you to be failing in your compliance because you appear to be misrepresenting your financial information.

Being off in the short term has profound effects on your accounting when it is used to its full extent.

Accounting is most valuable when you use it to project forward to determine if the path you are on is working. By letting you forecast financial information to come, you can make plans on how to manage your business for success in the long term. Being able to make projections as to where you want to be and use these to build out a budget that will get you there, this is one of the most beneficial aspects to bring accounting into your life. If you have faulty information then you will make shoddy projections that fail to be reflected by reality. In a way, this is an argument for combining bookkeeping and accounting together as a skill set you want to learn rather than accounting alone, but it is a truly powerful tool for entrepreneurs to master.

Finally, don't forget that the financial statements you generate through accounting need to be filed with the appropriate authorities such as the Registrar of Companies. If your company is large enough to be on the stock exchange then this will mean even more paperwork to be done. Part of accounting is simply learning who needs to receive what paperwork and then generating it for them. This is probably the most important part of the process but it is also the least exciting. Once you learn how to tackle this, it is a piece of cake.

Accounting is important because it gives you valuable information and allows you to legally continue running your business. Really can't get away with running a business without a bit of accounting. Rather than spend a bunch of money to get someone else to do it, this book offers you the benefit of taking it into your own hands to keep your operating costs even lower!

The Big Two: Financial and Managerial Accounting

When it comes to accounting there are a lot of different types, but businesses are going to have two that pop up with a greater frequency. These are financial accounting and managerial accounting. These can be thought of as external and internal accounting. Financial accounting is the external one as it focuses on the financial information that is necessary for legal reasons. This is contrasted with managerial accounting which focuses on financial information for use within the company.

Financial Accounting: Financial accounting is the recording and grouping of financial information, such as transactions, into statements. These statements are used to provide information about your company's finances to people outside of the company. These could be creditors or banks looking to see if they should loan you money. This could also be to investors who are looking to get involved with your company. It is incredibly important that you keep records of this sort.

Financial accounting requires the use of a chart of accounts. This is a record of the financial transactions that your company has had and it is created in order to store financial information that can be used and referenced later on. There are certain rules and regulations in place in regards to how your chart of accounts and the information therein works. Financial statements that make their way into the accounts are released to the users of those accounts and lawsuits related to false financial statements are a common practice. It is extremely important that the information you use in financial accounting is always accurate.

One of the ways that this is achieved is by using an accounting framework such as the GAAP or the IFRS. We talk more about these in chapter three when we discuss accounting principles, but what is important to understand here is that these play a role in financial accounting and they help to shape the way that we create our statements. Whether or not you are a for-profit or a nonprofit organization will make a difference in which one you use and how you make your statements, but both nonprofits need to generate financial statements just as much as for-profits do.

As mentioned previously, those companies which are publicly-held and desire to sell shares through the stock exchange need to go through additional steps with their financial accounting. Publicly traded shares must comply with the regulations as set out by the Securities

8

and Exchange Commission or SEC. This is an extra set of hoops that need to be jumped through but most companies aren't going to start out with shares to sell and so it is often only a concern for larger companies. However, their statements and compliance do fall into the realm of financial reporting and are worth keeping in mind going forward.

Managerial Accounting: Also known as management accounting, this form of accounting is focused entirely on the processing reports and data that will be used internally. This accounting covers the type of information that a manager needs to make informed decisions about daily operations, hence the name. Because it is used for internal use rather than external accountability, managerial accounting is more likely to be a little bit different everywhere you go. The information that is important for a particular company will be the focal point for reports and those that are less important to your company may be the most important to another. This results in a lot more variety in managerial accounting when compared to financial accounting.

One key point of managerial accounting is variance reports. This is the reporting on the difference between a projection and a measured result. This can happen on day-to-day cycles, weekly, monthly, or quarterly cycles. While it is an important element of managerial accounting it is far from the only thing it covers.

Managerial accounting also deals with tracking and reporting on cash at hand, budgeting of capital funds, recording accurate inventory, ensuring that transfer pricing analyses and project profitability reports are generated. Pretty much any kind of report that can be useful for use within the company will find some reflection in managerial accounting.

You may learn a system of managerial accounting that works great for your company. Since it's internal, you don't need to follow any type of guideline when it comes to these reports. It is important, however, to keep in mind that internal and external accounting is completely different. You must follow guidelines when reporting outside of your company. Because you end up needing to follow guidelines no matter what, it can be a smart idea to try to keep your managerial accounting as close to the guidelines as possible. This simply helps to keep everything looking the same when it comes time to read the information and this has the effect of reducing possible errors.

Other Kinds of Accounting

I bet there are lots of people out there that didn't realize there was more to accounting than just the financial and managerial flavors. Accounting is one of those topics that everyone thinks they know and few actually do. There are actually a bunch of different types of accounting but they're not as important to us in our discussions throughout the book so we'll only look at them briefly here.

Cost Accounting: Cost accounting actually falls into the realm of managerial accounting but it is worth noting here, too. This form of accounting focuses on keeping track of the total cost of production a company has accrued through the assessing of fixed costs and variable costs.

Forensic Accounting: Forensic accounting is a field of accounting that seems a bit like a private investigator's job. In accounting you are mostly working from all the data and just putting it together in fascinating ways. In forensic accounting, you lack all of the necessary financial records you would need and so it is up to you to go through the available data to figure out what is missing.

This type of accounting is used by investigators to try to take down illegal businesses. By spotting financial records that are fraudulent, investigators can either press charges or gain insight into criminal operations in this manner. But forensic accounting isn't always used to catch crooks. Sometimes the reason that records are missing can be entirely innocent, such as when a business catches fire and loses some of or all of their records.

Most businesses won't ever hire a forensic accountant and if they do then it is likely that they are working on a freelance or a consulting basis. This is because forensic accountants aren't useful 99% of the time. When they are, they're one of the most useful people you could ever meet.

Governmental Accounting: This is a field of accounting that has a tight grip on the resources being accounted for. It also focuses on breaking down activities into different sections to make it crystal clear how the various resources involved are being used. However, it is unlikely that you will ever need to worry about government accounting for your business because it is pretty much exclusively used by the government, though the levels do differ. Local governments to the country-wide government all make use of this style.

Governmental bodies have their own specific needs when it comes to accounting. While we've briefly discussed the idea of accounting standards and how making them so widely accepted has helped reduce accounting errors, this whole conversation goes out the window when we discuss governmental accounting. This type of accounting uses entirely different standards from what your business or nonprofit uses. They go through the GASB or the Governmental Accounting Standards Board.

We could dive deep into governmental accounting and fill out the rest of this chapter but this would be meaningless to you. The important takeaway here is that the standards of governmental accounting are different from those you'll be using. If you want to learn more about governmental accounting then you are likely considering a job as a government accountant and you'll want to seek out more in-depth information and education.

Public Accounting: This is more a description of a business' services than a particular kind of accounting. Public accounting is the term used to describe a business that can be hired to provide accounting services. What this means exactly is going to be dependent on the situation at hand. A public accountant could be hired to look after your tax returns. In fact, this is the most common use of public accounting. But they could also be hired to help you prepare your financial statements for external use or they could help you audit your company or clients. Another extremely common service they are hired to provide is simple consulting services to help you understand how to integrate a new accounting system on your computers, or perhaps they are needed to help with some forensic accounting to find information that has gone missing.

A public accountant is going to have rules and restrictions surrounding what information they can use, what information they aren't allowed to see, and what services they can offer. One of the major restrictions which is encountered quite often is centered around auditing. There are a bunch of obstacles that must be overcome in order for a public accountant to be able to help with auditing, such as having to register their accounting company with the Public Company Accounting Oversight Board or PCAOB. This registration comes with annual fees and requirements in terms of paperwork that must be completed. These costs are simply too much for many smaller accounting firms to pay.

A public accounting firm can only truly run in an economically sound way by employing lots of certified public accountants. By having enough of them, they will be able to afford the licencing to perform audits. The certification for public accountants used to be directly related to their ability to perform an audit but it has since been expanded to be seen as a sign of a highly qualified accountant. This means that you can expect to pay more to a certified public accountant than an uncertified one. Many small businesses find that the cost of a public accountant is just too dang high.

Which is why I argue that you should learn these skills for yourself. That way you can save your money and put it into the projects that will benefit your business' growth the most.

Tax Accounting: We come, at last, to tax accounting. This is the one that most people understand, at least in a basic way. You need to follow rules and regulations for reporting the assets and liabilities from your business. It doesn't follow any of the accounting frameworks that we've previously mentioned but instead it replies on the Internal Revenue Code or IRC. A tax accountant uses the information you've provided them to generate the amount of taxable income you've had. Tax accounting is pretty complicated because the number on your financial records isn't necessarily the final number they're worried about. They have to look at assets, reporting rules, and all sorts of other information in order to come up with the final taxable number.

This can have a positive result or a negative one. I personally saw the power of a good tax accountant this year. When it came time to do my taxes, I did a quick job of them and handed them off to a friend of mine who does tax accounting for a living. With the numbers I had provided, I was expecting to pay about $500 in taxes when all was said and done. He took one look at them, shuffled things a little bit and made me $800 back from the government. I don't know how he did it, I still haven't had a chance to ask because he's been as busy as I am, but that is the power of a good tax accountant. While you can learn to do your taxes yourself, it can really be worth getting a professional's eyes on them when you are just starting out. Just make sure to ask lots of questions so you can understand what they've done to help you so you can use it for yourself later.

The Differences Between Bookkeeping and Accounting

Bookkeeping is the process of recording financial transactions and keeping track of everything. Accounting works off of this tracked information to analyze, report, summarize, and interpret what the numbers from bookkeeping tells us. Both of these skills need to be used together in order to have the best results but many people think they are the same thing. This is especially understandable in our current age where accounting software often doubles as bookkeeping softwares. We'll look more at the similarities in a moment. First, let's explore the differences between these two.

The first major difference comes in the form of the definition of each field. This may seem obvious but it can help us to get a better understanding. Bookkeeping is about the identifying and recording of transactions. Accounting is about the interpreting and communicating of this financial information. One way of thinking of this is that bookkeeping is the process of writing a book while accounting would be the process of reviewing that book. Or for another metaphor, bookkeeping is checking the supplies and preparing the recipe for supper while accounting is the act of putting all of the ingredients together. Both bookkeeping and accounting directly invoke each other but this invocation is not the same as an equivalence.

The next major difference is key. Bookkeeping is about the recording of data. This means that the information that bookkeeping focuses on is plain. There is nothing fancy about it in the least, there are no great discoveries waiting in it. Bookkeeping is in no way a skill that lends itself to making decisions. But the data from the bookkeeping can be given over to an accountant who will shape that data into all sorts of different reports and these reports are the single-most useful tool that a manager or CEO has at their disposal when making decisions about their business. Likewise, this shows that the objective of the bookkeeper is to, well, keep the books up to date. The accountant's goal is to make sense of the books to see what they tell about the direction the company is headed.

Bookkeeping does not require any special skills. In fact, if you have some paper and a pencil then you can start keeping your books easily. Simply jot down everything you spend and every dollar you make. You don't even need to worry about sorting them out or weighing them against each other yet. All of this comes from the accounting side of things where you need to understand what you are doing to properly fill out reports and financial statements. It is these statements which will help you to understand whether you're making money or losing money in the long term. Similarly, bookkeeping doesn't analyze the data it brings in. It doesn't place it into a report or a statement but nor does it really try any form of analyzing. It is all about the recording.

So there are the major differences between bookkeeping and accounting. For many years these differences represented quite a large gap between the two practices. A company would hire a bookkeeper and an accountant. For example, my father has worked as a bookkeeper for decades and when he first started out that was all he did. As technology has advanced, the need for bookkeeping has been met by software developers. Now the role of the bookkeeper and the accountant are much closer together than they ever were before and my father no longer finds himself working alongside accountants, but rather he is one these days. So while this section is to highlight the differences between these two, it would be a disservice not to see how these two are growing more similar all the time.

The Slow Merging of Bookkeeping and Accounting

As technology advances, the distinction between bookkeeping and accounting will continue to fade away. This is seen first in the way that software has taken over many of the functions of the bookkeeper. Likewise, some bookkeeping software has taken over some of the responsibilities of the accountant, such as being able to create financial statements. This makes sense when you consider that the accountant must work from the information the bookkeeper has provided. Accounting used to be done by hand, with accountants needing to remember how to do each and every part. Accounting software now takes care of the majority of the calculations based on what you input.

This has led to the decline of bookkeeping as a career because it is slowly becoming obsolete. You used to need a bookkeeper to look over all the various accounts and make sure that transactions were logged in each one accordingly. But, again, technology now manages a large portion of this. Programs like QuickBooks have revolutionized the business world by giving the tools for bookkeeping and accounting over to the everyman. Are you a freelancer? Then you can take care of all your bookkeeping and accounting needs by spending five dollars a month for QuickBooks self-employed service. A larger but still small company could easily find all their needs met by spending $15-$25 a month for the more advanced QuickBooks service.

You know what has really caused this merging obsolescence more than anything else? The invention of smartphones. Now everyone has the ability to keep a tiny computer in their pocket that can be loaded with all of the software they need to run their business, from logging employee hours to keeping track of the books and even generating reports. Everything you need can fit into your pocket. When you realize this is the case it becomes extremely hard to justify hiring an employee to take care of bookkeeping or accounting for you. It is only as your company grows that it starts to become more appealing.

Do you need a bookkeeper *and* an accountant? Not really. Most accountants looking for employment these days will include bookkeeping on their resume because they understand that technology has fused these two roles. They might be different from one another but that doesn't mean they need to be handled by different people. Throughout the remainder of this book, we're going to be speaking about accounting, but often we will be bringing in elements of bookkeeping because of how tightly related they are. This would likely make an old-school accountant (or bookkeeper) angry, but it is a reflection of the technological times we live in.

Chapter Summary

- Accounting is a wider field than many realize, with different types of accounting that can vary wildly from each other.

- Accounting is one of the most important aspects of running a business.

- There are laws that must be followed when it comes to accounting, otherwise your business will not be legal.

- Accountants generate financial statements which give a sense of where the company is currently but they can also be used to project into the future to estimate where the company is headed.

- Accounting takes the guessing out of your finances and lets you get solid numbers down in a form that you can play around with to test out different strategies before adapting them.

- Accounting isn't bookkeeping but many accounting programs now cover bookkeeping issues, too.

- The two big types of accounting that we are concerned with in this book are financial accounting and managerial accounting.

- Financial accounting is concerned with recording and grouping financial information into statements. These statements are useful for investors to get a sense of how your company is doing and where it is spending its money.

- The financial statements that we generate in financial accounting are required by law and it is extremely important to ensure that the information in them is accurate.

- Information is kept accurate and easy to read by the use of an accounting framework like GAAP or IFRS, depending on where your business is located.

- Companies that are publicly traded have more paperwork to fill out in their financial accounting than those that aren't.

- Managerial accounting is a type of accounting that processes reports and financial data for use within the organization. Because managerial accounting is undertaken for internal use only, there is no specific accounting framework that must be used.

- Managerial accounting makes good use of variance reports, reports that show the difference between a projection and a measured result. This helps to give a sense of how the company is performing compared to how it was expected to perform.

- While financial accounting and managerial accounting are the two most important for beginners to learn, there are all sorts of other types of accounting, too.

- Cost accounting is a form of accounting that keeps tracks of the total cost of production that a company has built up.

- Forensic accounting is a fascinating field of accounting that combines accounting with detective work. Forensic accountants recreate books and records using partial or obscured data. Many work in some form of investigative capacity but others specialize in recovery such as when financial records are lost to technical error or in an accident like a fire.

- Governmental accounting is a form of accounting that is used exclusively by the government and it can have quite a variety of unique rules to it based on location. Most businesses will never have to worry about governmental accounting.

- Public accounting is more a name for a service rather than a style of accounting. If a firm hires accountants out to the public or to other businesses then these accountants would be considered to work in public accounting. Ever since 2002 there have been more rules than ever about what a public accountant can and can't do and there is lots of paperwork that a public accountant must have in order to legally work in the field.

- Because public accounting can be such an expensive career path, it is unlikely that you will encounter small-scale public accounting firms. It makes more sense economically for these firms to function at a larger-scale.

- Tax accounting is the form of accounting that learns tax law. A good tax accountant can save you lots of money by knowing how to properly claim expenses and juggle numbers.

- Bookkeeping is primarily concerned with keeping track of the accounts and logging all the necessary transactions. Accounting is concerned with generating financial statements and making projections about the future of the company.

- Accounting and bookkeeping go hand-in-hand, with bookkeeping being necessary for the accounting department to work their magic. Small companies will find that they can combine these two jobs together to save money.

In the next chapter you will learn the definitions behind some of the most important accounting terms. We'll cover all of the basics from assets to liabilities and from financial statements to the accounting equation. These basic concepts will crop up again and again throughout the book so it is important that we cover them in-depth before we get too much further.

CHAPTER TWO

ACCOUNTING BASICS

How much do you know about accounting already? Can you describe the accounting equation? Can you define the difference between your company's assets and liabilities? What about a financial statement? We've mentioned them quite a few times already throughout the book but do you really understand what we mean by them?

In this chapter we're going to work our way through these questions and more. This chapter can be considered almost like a glossary for the discussion to come. Without tackling these questions we won't be able to continue forward on the same page. And if there is one thing that I want us to share, it is the page that we are on. So if you were able to answer all of the questions in the previous paragraph then this chapter isn't going to cover anything you don't yet know, but if you struggled with even one of them then you'll want to stick around.

What is the Accounting Equation?

The accounting equation is a bit of an intimidating name. Yes, it does mean that there will be math to tackle. Though this shouldn't come as a surprise considering that we're discussing financial information, after all. The accounting equation is basically the foundation of any double-entry accounting setup. You see the accounting equation on your balance sheet where it is used to weigh your assets against your liabilities and shareholders' equity.

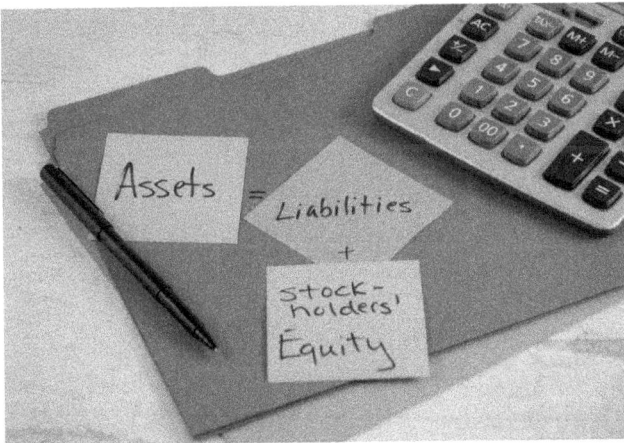

The accounting equation's formula is quite simple:

Assets = Liabilities + Owner's Equity

To calculate the accounting equation you need to find all of your company's assets on the balance sheet for the period you're looking at. Next you must add up all of the liabilities that the company has. The liabilities should have their own listing on the balance sheet. The third step is to locate the total of the shareholders' equity and combine this to the total from your liabilities. This finally gives you the last number, as combining the total from liabilities to the total from shareholders' equity will give you the total assets you have.

This simple equation is the cornerstone of accounting. You need to understand assets, liabilities, and stockholders' equity to get a full picture of the importance of this equation.

What are Assets?

An asset is anything that you own that has a value or that can be converted into money. Every company has its own assets but so does every individual. Assets are often used in order to create a cash flow at a later date, such as when you purchase a patent or a piece of equipment that you need in order to run your projects. For example, a lawn mower is a piece of equipment that counts as an asset. You could always sell it if you need to but it will make you cash down the road when you start to use it to mow lawns for your clients.

Personal assets are typically valued either at the individual level or at the household level for families. These include cash and cash equivalents and this can include the cash you have on hand and as well as the cash in your bank account. Any property you own counts as an asset and if you have a house or other building on that land then this also counts as an asset. Certain personal possessions count, such as vehicles, boats, furniture, jewelry, collectibles, and more. However, it is this category of assets that makes for the most confusing calculation as there are strict laws around which items can and cannot be counted as assets. Less difficult to understand is that your investments, all of them from mutual funds to bonds and retirement plans, count as assets. All of these assets are combined to give you a number. This number has your liabilities subtracted from it in order to give you what is called your net worth.

A business asset is anything of value that your business owns rather than you yourself. If you drive your car to work then that car is a personal asset but if you have a company car then that would be an asset of the company and not one of yours. Business assets can include machinery like this, as well as property, the raw materials used for making your goods, and those goods that you have in inventory already. These are all tangible assets. Intangible assets are things such as any intellectual property your company owns, the royalties they receive from previous projects, and any patents you have registered. The balance sheet will show all of your company's assets, as well as whether they have been paid for already or whether they are under debt.

Assets are further broken down into current assets and fixed assets. A current asset is one that you can turn into cash within a year. Cash is a current asset, since you don't need to turn it into anything to begin, but so too are cash equivalents like treasury bills or bonds. Marketable securities, accounts receivables, and your inventory are all considered to be current assets. Fixed assets are those which are used in the production of goods or in the process of the services you offer. These are things like vehicles, machinery, buildings, land, furniture, and the like. These items could technically be converted into cash at a short notice if need be but they aren't accounted for in this manner. For example, you could sell a building in a week if you were lucky but you can't guarantee that you can achieve this so it is a fixed asset rather than a current one.

In order to fully appreciate assets, you need to remember that liabilities interact with them such as when your net worth is calculated by taking your liabilities out of assets. To see why liabilities are subtracting from your personal assets to make your net worth but are added with owner's equity to equal a company's assets, you're just going to have to keep reading.

What Are Liabilities?

Liabilities are one of the places that people begin to get confused when it comes to accounting. Assets are pretty easy to understand as they are basically possessions. Whether you possess something or your company does, the owner of that possession can view it as an asset. It doesn't cover items with sentimental value such as a seashell you were gifted by a loved one, so not every possession is an asset, but most people don't have any trouble with wrapping their head around this one.

Liabilities are different. Liabilities are what you owe. They tend to be dealt with over time rather than straight away. Liabilities can be settled by exchanging money, goods, or services. If I write a book for a company that is going to pay me at a later date then this promise of pay is a liability (though it must be noted in a legal fashion, otherwise there is not a real liability but rather an informal one). Liabilities as noted on the balance sheet include things like loans and mortgages, premiums, and deferred revenues. Because they deal with something that isn't really solid but more like a conceptual category of information, it can be quite difficult to sort it all out. This is made even more confusing when you take into account that your liability can change when you get married or start having children.

The most common liability is a financial liability. If you hired a consultant and have received their bill but haven't paid it yet then this becomes a financial liability. You are liable for the amount you owe. Basically, a liability is an obligation to settle at a later date. The later date part is important. If you paid your gardener in cash for their services then this is a cost, not a liability. But if they gave you their bill on Friday and you plan to pay it on Sunday then you have a liability for those two days. This is a very, very short-term liability. Most liabilities that accrue through your business will be divided into short-term or long-term liabilities. Short-term liabilities are those that should be cleared in less than a year and long-term liabilities are those that are expected to take a year or more.

Liabilities are common in pretty much every business. If you are running a store then you will be dealing in cash transactions with your customers and so it is unlikely that liabilities will arise from there. But you are likely to be liable to manufacturers and suppliers you work with to get your raw materials. It is in this part of your business that the liabilities really pop up. If you aren't running a store but are providing your goods to other stores to be sold then chances are you are the one who will be expecting a pay and so you'll be the only handing out liabilities.

So liabilities are promises to pay. When you are calculating your own net worth, you don't calculate what you still owe. Your business must take this into account in the accounting equation or it will result in misrepresented financial information that can cause legal issues you'd rather avoid.

What is Stockholders' Equity?

Stockholders' equity is the phrase we use to refer to the assets that a company has available for shareholders once all of the company's liabilities are paid for. A stockholder is of course any individual that owns one or more shares in a company's capital stock, these shares are primarily common stock for most companies within the United States. Stockholders are separate from a company and thus they are considered to have limited liability in regards to the company. Common stockholders will help to elect a corporation's board of directors and they typically vote on issues such as mergers.

A company's stockholders' equity is typically calculated by totalling all of the company's assets and subtracting its liabilities. Another form of calculating a company's stockholders' equity is by totaling the share capital and retained earnings and subtracting any treasury shares, which is the term used to describe stock that a company has purchased back from shareholders. Stockholders' equity can be used as a way of viewing a company's success. If a company has a positive stockholders' equity then that company is doing well, or at least managing to get by. When a company has a negative stockholders' equity then we are often right to guess that the company will be declaring bankruptcy or folding in the near future.

Stockholders' equity begins with the money that is invested in the beginning through those that purchase shares. This is then combined with the retained earnings the company has managed to acquire through their operations. The initial investment is extremely important in the beginning, as that is where most of the money to launch the business comes from. The longer a business has been functioning, the less important this initial investment becomes while the retained earnings continue to grow. Basically, stockholders purchase into your company with the expectation that the business will make money. Retained earnings are expected to grow, thus making back the initial investment that is represented by purchasing shares.

As a company continues to grow, they often end up engaging in share buybacks to create treasury shares. Everyone that has a share in the company is entitled to a portion of the company's earnings, typically in what is called a dividend. Since every stockholder represents more money leaving the company each quarter in dividend payments, it is often beneficial for a company with large retained earnings to purchase back shares by buying out a stockholders' shares. This process of buying back shares creates treasury shares and, while these still count towards a company's total issued shares, treasury shares do not count as outstanding. This means that the company does not need to take these shares into account when paying their quarterly dividends or when they are calculating the earnings per share. Treasury shares can always be sold at a later date when the company has a need for raising further capital or they can be retired to no longer have any value.

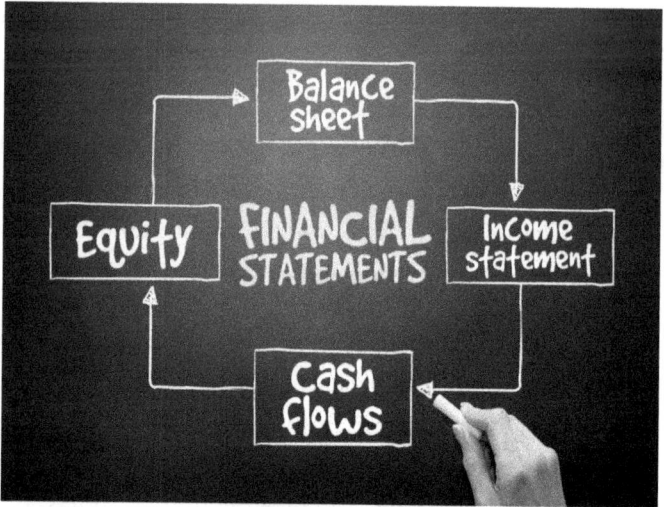

What Are Financial Statements?

Financial statements are simply written and logged records that each company is required to have in order to show what activities they have been taking part in and how those activities have performed financially. Financial statements are neutral documents which convey information on the reality of a company's financials and therefore they are quite boring as there is no spinning of the numbers or creating a narrative of the company's progress. They represent a company when it has been boiled down to the purely numerical.

Financial statements are extremely important as various governmental bodies require them to be provided by scheduled dates and they can be audited at any time. Audits are one of those terms that everyone understands to be bad but they really aren't. An audit is simply the process whereby an authority or someone acting on behalf of an authority performs an official inspection of your company's accounts. Audits are most often performed by someone working independently of your company, unless of course we are talking about an internal audit in which case the information is less official and more important for making informed decisions and catching errors before financial reporting. Audits are often performed by the government in order to ensure that you are being honest to investors and paying the appropriate taxes.

Financial statements are used to judge how well a company is performing and to make informed estimates regarding how the company will grow financially in the future. Financial statements come in several forms such as balance sheets, cash flow statements, and income statements. It must be noted here that financial statements aren't the end-all be-all documents that many seem to think they are. While they are neutral documents, there is room to interpret the data therein in different ways and it isn't uncommon for one investor to read a financial statement and arrive at a completely different opinion on the company's success when compared to another investor. This flexibility of interpretation may be seen as a positive in the realm of something like literature and narrative but it is a limitation in regards to financial performance and it is often best to provide investors with more information through additional documents, like road maps that show which direction the company is headed.

As financial statements are such an integral part of accounting we will be looking at them in-depth in chapter four where we will speak at length about balance sheets, cash flow statements, income statements, and statements of retained earnings.

What Are Taxes?

Taxes are one of those things about life that we can't escape from, like breathing or dying. Okay, maybe they aren't quite as bad as that last one, but there's more than enough sayings equating the two. Taxes are fees that the government levies on both individuals and businesses. By collecting taxes the government is then able to fund things like schools, hospitals, and the military, as well as smaller services such as roadwork.

Taxes come in many different forms. Income tax is placed on the money that an individual makes. Corporate taxes are collected from businesses. Sales tax is collected on many different goods at the point of sale. Property taxes are calculated and paid based on how much an owned piece of land and property is worth. Tariffs are taxes which are paid when importing goods and estate tax is calculated based on the value of a person's estate at the point of their death. We aren't going to be concerning ourselves too much with taxes throughout the book and this is the only point that we'll be mentioning many of these.

It is worth understanding corporate tax a little bit better, though. This tax is placed on the profit that your company makes, otherwise known as operating earnings. This is calculated by deducting expenses. The tax rate, as set by the government, is applied to the operating earnings to arrive at the amount your company owes in taxes. Because expenses are deducted before taxes are calculated there are some tricks that businesses use to reduce the amount of tax they need to pay. One well known example comes from Hollywood where film companies would purposefully make a movie that they knew was going to tank at the box office. If the movie made money for them then it would increase their earnings and thus increase the size of their taxes. But if they lose money on the movie then that was an expense that brings down their operating earnings so that they can land in a less expense tax bracket.

I do not recommend that newer companies try to play the system to this degree. It is likely to end you up in trouble, as the younger a company is the easier it is for expenses to get out of hand. Do keep in mind that the more you earn, the more you must pay. Sometimes it is best to push a profitable project a few weeks or even months down the road so that the profits aren't in yet when it comes time to calculate your taxes.

Chapter Summary

- The accounting equation is the foundation of any double-entry accounting system.

- The accounting equation is: **Assets = Liabilities + Owner's Equity**.

- We need to figure out what assets, liabilities, and owner's equity is in order to understand this equation. Each of these components makes up the basic building blocks of accounting.

- Assets are anything of value that can be turned into money. They can be used to create cash flow at a later date and include things from the company's actual on-hand cash to equipment that allows you to generate income at a later date.

- Personal assets are something that every individual owns and they can be looked at both on a personal level as well as on the level of a family for those who are married or have children.

- Personal assets include vehicles, boats, furniture, jewelry, collectibles, and more. They also include investments, mutual funds, bonds, and retirement plans. All of these assets are combined together, at which point your liabilities are subtracted, and you end up at your net worth.

- A business' assets are items that have been bought by the business rather than by any of its employees. A work car, equipment for production, the property and raw materials for the store, any stock already in inventory, all of these are examples of the assets a business owns.

- Tangible assets are like those we just mentioned but intangible assets include items like any intellectual property the company owns or any royalties it receives.

- Assets are divided into current assets and fixed assets.

- Current assets are assets which can be turned into cash within a year.

- Fixed assets are any assets that take longer than a year to turn into cash such as property.

- Liabilities are what you owe and they are typically dealt with over time by paying them back slowly. However, they typically increase before expansions as you raise or borrow more money in order to grow the company. While everyone dreams of paying off all that they owe, it is very common for successful companies to never end up paying off all their liabilities at the same time.

- When you perform a service for someone and hand them their bill with a date for a later payment then they are liable to you for that money. These do not count as our liabilities when doing accounting for our company but rather a way to see how liabilities are gathered.

- Even stores that deal primarily in cash are likely to end up with some liabilities on their hands when dealing with manufacturers and supplies. They have a way of stacking up even when you don't expect them to.

- Stockholders' equity are the assets that a company has available after all the company's liabilities have been paid off. This doesn't mean that the liabilities themselves have been paid off but rather that we have added up all of our liabilities and then removed that much of our revenue to get the amount we have in stockholders' equity.

- A stockholder is any individual that has purchased shares in your company. This is most often done so that the stockholder can earn a dividend, a regular payment of part of the company's finances. The size of the dividend a person receives depends on how many shares they own and how much each share is worth.

- A company may have treasury shares. These are shares that they have purchased back from shareholders to keep for themselves. Treasury shares still count as issued shares but they don't require the company to pay any dividends.

- A company with a positive stockholders' equity is doing well while one with a negative stockholders' equity is probably going to fold in the near future.

- A company's retained earnings are added to the stockholders' equity and so it often begins with money from investors but it should continue to grow beyond investors through money retained from earnings.

- Financial statements are statements which convey information and hard data about a company's finances for a given period of time. They are neutral documents that give investors and government workers the ability to see your company's financial records without any obscuration.

- Financial statements are made following a set of standards which helps to keep everything looking the same for ease of reading.

- Financial statements must be kept and they must be honest. There are many laws surrounding what you cannot do with your financial statements and punishments are higher now than ever before.

- Taxes are fees that the government places on both individuals and businesses. There are all sorts of different taxes and how much a company pays depends on how the company does, how much it spends doing that and how much it earns.

- Taxes are used to improve the infrastructure of the county and to fund public works.

In the next chapter you will learn about the different frameworks that we use in order to keep our financial reports in legal order. These include the Generally Accepted Accounting Principles or the GAAP and the International Financial Reporting Standards or IFRS. Which of these you need to follow depends on whether you are running a nonprofit or a for-profit organization but both types of businesses need to follow these standards in order to ensure they are compliant, which is a whole new can of worms that we'll get into next.

CHAPTER THREE

ACCOUNTING PRINCIPLES

Now that we have an understanding of the basics it is time to turn our attention towards the principles of accounting. These range from the frameworks we use, such as GAAP or IFRS, to ideals such as the revenue recognition principle, the historical cost principle, the matching principle, the full disclosure principle, and the objectivity principle. As you'll see, a good framework covers these principles.

We will begin with these principles then move into our frameworks. This will have the effect of showing us what "good accounting" is and how we achieve it through either GAAP or IFRS. We'll compare GAAP and IFRS against each other to see how they are similar, how they differ, and what you need to know about using them. Finally, we'll close the chapter on a discussion of compliance within accounting.

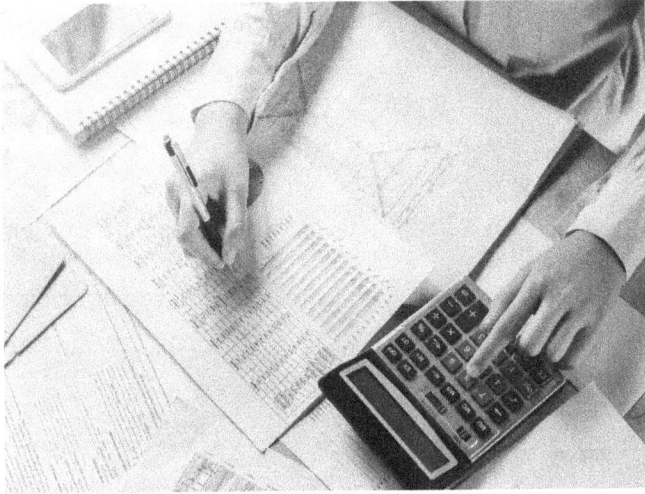

The Principles of Accounting

If you are going to run a business and keep everything legal and above the books then you absolutely must learn these principles and keep them in mind when doing your own accounting. A professional accountant will already know these and follow them closely, so you don't need to worry about a professional you hire messing them up. When you are learning to be your own accountant it is extremely easy to overlook these principles and end up causing errors and headaches down the road.

Never forget that the core of accounting, even more so than finances, is accurate and replicable reporting. I want to recommend that those learning accounting for the first time take extra caution when starting out. Don't just generate a single statement and call it a day. Go through the numbers a second time and generate the report again to make sure that the outcome is the same. This is not a principle of accounting that we'll be looking at but rather a principle for those beginning accounting.

So with that said let us dive into the key principles.

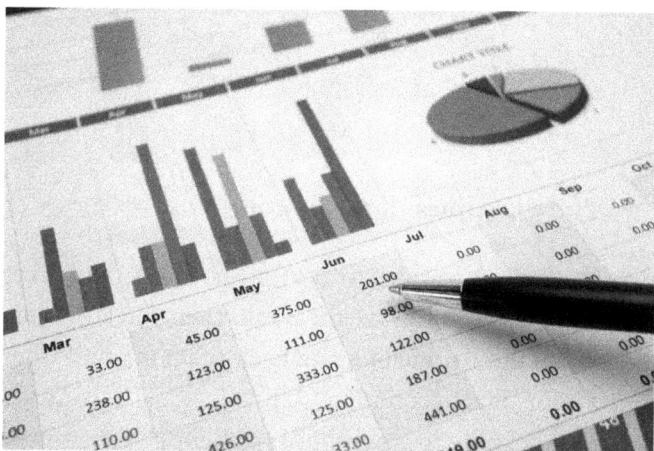

Revenue Recognition Principle: This principle is incredibly important, seems like common sense, and yet is often one of the those broken the most often. The revenue recognition principle informs us that we must recognize revenue as income. If you are running a coffee shop and you hand a customer their cup, the money they hand you is revenue. Revenue can come from selling goods or performing services. It can also come from sources like royalties or dividends.

For the most part you shouldn't have much trouble with understanding this principle. The hardest part of it comes from realizing just how easy it can be to break it. To use a personal example, I have a friend that runs a tattoo shop for a living who was training a new artist. As a new artist, he wasn't earning an income through the shop yet but rather they were training him at a loss with plans for future profits. He had to find his own clients and he couldn't charge them but he was getting hands-on training from professionals with thirty-plus years of experience. However, he had to be let go because he broke the revenue recognition principle and he opened the business up to a threat.

How did he do this? He took a $50 tip after a session. You might think that a tip isn't part of the business's revenue but it absolutely is. By taking the money and not informing the company, he unintentionally shoved them into illegal waters. There was no purchase and the service itself was free but by not reporting that tip the young artist broke the first principle of accounting. So it is important to keep your mind broad when you are considering revenue. It is always best to keep track of every single cent that comes into your company when it does, you can always remove them from your reporting later if it turns out that they are unnecessary.

Historical Cost Principle: This principle is applied to assets which a company has purchased at a cost. There are some assets which a company can acquire without paying anything. For example, pretend a well-known celebrity tweeted their praise of your services. This is great for marketing, it is fantastic for bringing in new customers, it is an asset. But it is not an asset in the way that accounting views assets and so it is irrelevant. Assets which cost money are important because they play directly into the historical cost principle.

When you purchase assets you must record the price they were purchased at. It is this price that will be used in your accounting. If the price changes (both higher or lower), it doesn't matter. You purchased the asset at the price you have recorded and it is this price that you will use for your accounting going forward. If you purchase additional assets at a different price then they must be recorded but the newly recorded price is carried forward.

This principle is important for keeping track of your finances. Say that one of your assets is a piece of technology that you purchased brand new. A few years later and the company is no longer producing that particular model. Collectors are now purchasing them at

an inflated price. Even if the average price is now ten times as much as it was when you bought it, you have to list it at the original price. This helps to keep your records in order but it can also be beneficial, as the company could now sell this asset and earn a much greater profit compared to what they were valued at holding onto the asset.

Matching Principle: The matching principle can be a harder one to understand. It took me a little while to wrap my head around it at first. The principle itself is quite simple, however, once you sort it out. What the matching principle is all about is making sure that your expenses are accounted for during the same period of time that the revenue they're connected to is claimed. This can be a little confusing because what if you purchased supplies months ago and just used them to sell something today? Would that earlier expense not be applied until now?

Actually, yes, but there's more to it. It is easier to consider this principle with an example. Let's say that your employees are paid once a month on a set day. On the 10th of every month, your employees are paid out the earnings that they have acquired through sales commissions or similar. If your employees make 10% commission and they have sold $50000 in the accounting period, they would be paid their 10% commission in the following month, outside of the accounting period in question. However, the income that expense comes out of is accounted for in the given month and this means so to must that payment. So while you haven't technically paid your employees that $5000 yet, you do need to count it in the same period because the income the expense is related to needs to be recorded.

This principle disregards the timing of payment and it disregards your real cash flow. That $5000 did not leave the company during this time period after all. What it does is narrow the focus onto the accrual of expenses and revenue from the period.

Keep in mind that the matching principle does not mean that every expense needs to be matched. There are expenses like rent that aren't related to your revenue and therefore there is nothing to match it to. Income itself has to be matched to expenses.

Also keep in mind that this needs to be compared against your inventory, too. If you sell 100 units of your most popular item then you would have to record the cost of goods for 100 units. But if in that same period you purchased 10 more units then your real cost of goods sold is 90 units. So making sure that your expenses for goods sold is a matter of balancing expenses, revenue, and inventory.

Full Disclosure Principle: Out of all the principles in this chapter, this is the one that is the easiest to explain. What the full disclosure principle tells us is that the financial statements we generate must be about conveying information to the reader. As the readers are going to most likely be either in the government or they're going to be your investors, it just makes sense to convey information to them. What is important here is that you also aren't using your financial statements to conceal information. This would be money laundering.

In order to achieve this principle, all you need to do is tell the truth. Do your best to follow the principles that we have been discussing and do your best to keep all of your records honest. Issues may come up in which you accidentally mess up on a financial statement. This can be a real pain but catching it and owning up to it will still let you follow this one. You might break it in the short term on accident but you show that you want to fix it and ensure that your company is run with full disclosure.

One of the ways that accountants have improved their accountability to offer an even fuller disclosure is to present their financial statements alongside notes. While it is not required, you are always more than welcome to append a note onto your statements. This can help you to explain what happened in the period and what those reading the statements are seeing. Just remember that these notes are meant to be used to increase your disclosure and thus your honesty. You could append notes and fill them full of lies to hide the truth but this would be illegal, immoral, and it would absolutely be concealing financial information and thus breaking the full disclosure principle.

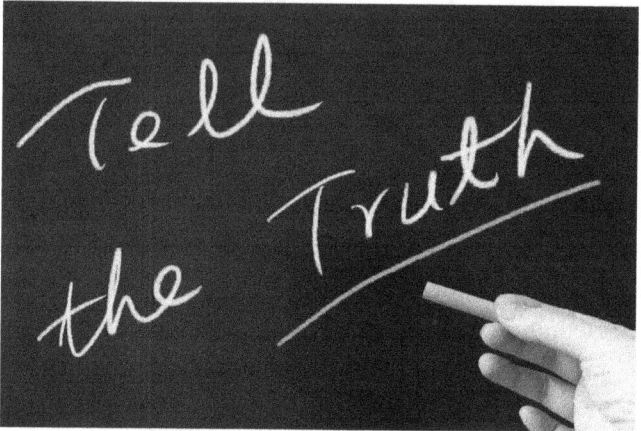

Objectivity Principle: The final principle that we'll look at before digging into GAAP and IFRS is the objectivity principle. This one is tightly tied to the full disclosure principle in that it is focused on keeping you as honest as you can be. In the full disclosure principle, that honesty is achieved by ensuring that all the relevant financial information is in place and accounted for. The objectivity principle relates less to the amount of information present and instead it looks towards the presentation of the data.

Financial statements are used in order to help project into the future. They give a sense of where the company is now and where they are going. But, as mentioned before, they have a limitation: they aren't concrete. Rather, financial statements can reveal different information to each person that reads them depending on what framework they want to view the information from. Because each person has their own bias as to what is or isn't a good sign, it can be easy to look at the data with our own perspective and want to make it reflect that. However, this would not be objective reporting but rather it would be subjective reporting and that has no place in the world of accounting.

By keeping the objectivity principle in mind we remember that the financial data we are reporting on must remain free from any personal bias. It must remain objective, not subjective. To do this we have to make sure that the data we use is verifiable. If we cannot verify where a number has come from then we have no use for it. Transactions need to have receipts and invoices and whatever documentation is necessary to prove it exists in a court of law. Of course you aren't going to need to go into a court of law if you are objective and commit to full disclosure, but you want to ensure that your financial statements are solid enough that they'd win any case.

If they aren't objective, they aren't solid.

G enerally
A ccepted
A ccounting
P rinciples

What is GAAP?

GAAP stands for Generally Accepted Accounting Principles. And guess what? You've just learned about the biggies. These standards are widely used, you might even say that they are generally used. Having seen the principles themselves, you should be able to understand why they are maintained. For example, telling the truth and making sure that everything can be tied to documentation is just smart.

Others, such as the matching principle, are a little bit more elusive. It's not that the matching principle really represents the best option for handling numbers. It's possible that it is but what matters is not whether or not it is the best but rather that it is the most generally used. This is where the GAAP really benefits accountants. If you are an accountant that has been hired to take over for a company then it is a lot easier to settle into the position since everything is laid out how it should be. In a way, using something besides the GAAP would be akin to doing your accounting in another language.

We covered the key principles but I would recommend reading the Federal Accounting Standards Advisory Board's handbook on accounting standards. The PDF is available for free online at fasab.gov/accounting-standards. There is a lot of information in their handbook and much of it will be irrelevant to you. It would be unrealistic for a beginner in accounting to read the whole book. It is better to instead use your electronic search tools to find those sections dealing with the topics your company handles.

The GAAP has many topics that fall under its purview, too. These cover assets, derivatives, equity, expenses, the presentation of your financial statements, foreign currency, fair value, revenue, leases, hedging, and more. This wide range of topics means it is best to assume that a particular item is discussed in the standards. It might not be, but if you assume that it is and quickly search the document, you will find that this is the safer approach while are still figuring out which elements apply to your situation.

The GAAP is not the only standards guide when it comes to accounting. There is also the IFRS, so let's take a quick look at that.

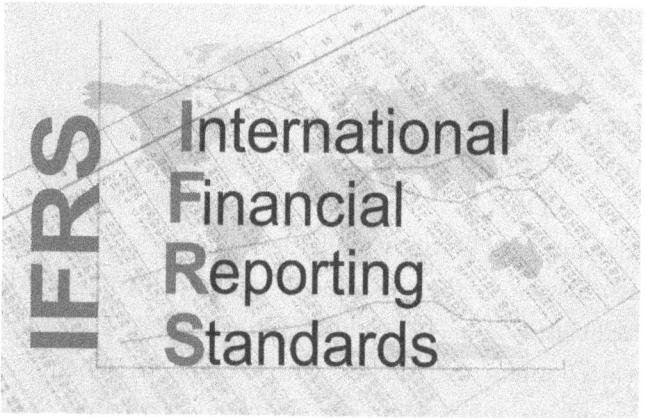

What is IFRS?

The answer to that question is the International Financial Reporting Standards. These standards are looser than the standards of the GAAP. They're also used in most countries. They deal more with the principles around accounting rather than with rules. There are a lot of rules in the GAAP, which is why it is good to become familiar with the search feature when dealing with them. This results in the IFRS being much easier to deal with.

GAAP vs. IFRS

The GAAP has been around longer and this means it is a much more comprehensive and complete set of standards in comparison. However, the GAAP is mostly used in the US while the IFRS is used around the world. If you are in the US then you should worry about following the rules as laid out in the GAAP. If you are located anywhere else then you will want to familiarize yourself more with the IFRS but keep in mind that you still might have to learn the GAAP.

IFRS approaches standardization of financial reporting through a system of standards. This means that it follows principles rather than rules. The principles we looked at in the first half of this chapter are important enough to set up the concept for what we are trying to achieve when reporting but there are many more rules in the GAAP.

While the International Accounting Standards Board doesn't actually make the GAAP, they are extremely influential in the way that it forms. They have no legal power over it whatsoever but when they set new standards they tend to be worked into multiple countries' standards. The new standard might go through a process of interpretation in which it may change or be slightly altered in order to be adapted. This in turn leads to the new standard helping to alter what a particular country's generally accepted accounting principles are.

But in the US, IFRS is irrelevant. The American GAAP are set by the Financial Accounting Standards Board and that's that. There have been movements for the US to switch to IFRS and the Securities and Exchange Commission have looked into it on certain occasions but they repeatedly turn down the concept. So for the time being, those in the US need to worry only about learning GAAP.

What is Compliance in Accounting?

Compliance means exactly what it sounds like. Rather than trying to break laws or go against the GAAP, you comply with the law and the standards that you are required to. Basically it just means that you will tell the truth, do it in a way that proves you are telling the truth, and thereby remain legal and compliant. This is done so that we never end up on the wrong side of a governmental body such as the SEC.

Famously, the Sarbanes-Oxley Act was put into place in the early 2000s. There were a ton of corporate scandals by that point, many of which arose directly from the way they handled their accounting. In order to reduce the amount of scandals and increase the level of compliance overall, this act was composed of eleven titles. Each of these titles make clear what is required for compliance.

Title 1: The first title brought the Public Company Accounting Oversight Board into existence. This board has the responsibility of keeping watch over the accounting done by firms that offer auditing services to companies that are traded publicly. This board also has the power to discipline companies which are failing to live up to the new processes for compliance with audits that came with the creation of the PCAOB.

Title 2: This title was created in order to reduce conflicts of interest that arose from auditing firms. Firms that were providing auditing were found to also be doing consulting work with the companies that they had been hired to audit. This created a conflict of interest that was completely transparent when brought to light in various scandals. In order to prevent this from happening, this title put standards of compliance in place for external auditors.

Title 3: Now we move into the responsibility of the corporation. The senior executives of a company are now explicitly held accountable for the accuracy of the financial numbers that the corporation reports. If the numbers are wrong and legal action is taken then it is now the CEO's fault. This means that those who are higher up at the company can't pass off responsibility (or blame) to those working beneath them.

Title 4: This title directly increased the principle of full disclosure to set rules in place as to what counted as disclosure and how it was to be provided.

Title 5: No matter how many rules you put in place there is always the chance of a conflict of interest passing through. This title was chosen to prevent conflicts of interest within the world of securities analysts. Now analysts are required by law to disclose any conflicts of interest they might have, that they know of. This title was chosen to help restore the public's confidence in securities analysts. Keep in mind, however, that the phrasing makes it clear that these conflicts are knowable. If a conflict of interest that was unknowable arises then it does not violate this. The best course of action in regards to compliance is to immediately own up to the conflict when it becomes clear.

Title 6: While the previous title required securities analysts to reveal their conflicts of interest, this title sets out how those professionals who work in securities are to act. This title was closely tied to the previous title as both were chosen in order to improve the public's confidence in securities professionals. But another component of this title was making it crystal clear what kind of authority the SEC has over securities analysts. If the SEC needs to, it was made clear that they have the power to discipline analysts. They can even bar them from practicing if they are found to be willfully conflicting with compliance practices.

Title 7: This title required the SEC and the Comptroller General to run a series of studies and make their findings public. Rather than any single topic, the studies they ran covered a range of discussions that ranged from how consolidating public accounting firms would play out to how investment banks factored into the major accounting scandals of the time. Other studies were performed as part of this title, thus completing its purpose. These studies were meant to give those in places of power, as well as investors, a clearer sense of what was happening within the world of corporate accounting.

Title 8: This title is sometimes called the Corporate and Criminal Fraud Act of 2002 and it's a pretty important act to be aware of. One of the problems with compliance was that the laws surrounding it were unclear. What exactly counted as obscuring information to give the illusion of compliance? And with all of these major companies like Enron creating large and well-documented scandals, why didn't anyone come forth sooner?

The problem here is that what could be played off as accidental and what counted as interference in terms of compliance was loosely defined. Furthermore, there wasn't a clear guideline as to what the penalties of these actions would be. What was known at the time, or at least most employees suspected, was that to speak out about what they were seeing would cost their jobs. They were right, too. But this title put in new penalties for interference and created protections for those who are willing to speak out about white collar crime when they encounter it.

Title 9: Speaking of white collar crime, this title also goes by the name of the White Collar Crime Penalty Enhancement Act of 2002. Corporate officers that failed to ensure that their financial reporting was certifiable and replicable now can have criminal charges placed against them. This ties this title closely to the corporate responsibility of title three. Along with increasing who is to be held accountable, this title also increased the penalties for crimes of this type and it especially increased them where conspiracies are concerned. It is a criminal offense to mess up through negligence but it is extremely damaging to be shown to be part of a conspiracy to commit white-collar crime.

Title 10: This title is the easiest of them all to understand. It's also the shortest. Simply put, the CEO of the company must sign every tax return related to the company. What this means is that the CEO of the company is agreeing, through their signature, with the information they are seeing. This means they had to not only have it sent to them so that they could look over it but that they had to physically indicate that they did.

With this title, there is no way for a CEO to say that they weren't aware of what was happening. Either they weren't aware and thus are showing that they are running things extremely poorly and they should not be left in charge, or they are showing that they knew there was a problem and still signed over their information anyway and that points towards conspiracy.

Title 11: The final title is known as the Corporate Fraud Accountability Act of 2002. This made committing fraud on a corporate level a criminal offense. This act also made tampering with financial records into a criminal offense, complete with information on how to sentence these crimes. Furthermore, this act also gave the SEC the ability to freeze transactions which it suspects could be problematic. Financial transactions that seem unusual or larger than normal can be frozen in order to be investigated.

The freezing of transactions comes with pros and cons. For the law-abiding company, a frozen payment is a hassle. It needs to get sorted out and this takes time. This law is troublesome in this case, but when it comes to companies that are trying to succeed at a scam then it can be invaluable. By freezing a transaction, the SEC has a better ability to investigate it as it is still "current." In contrast, a transaction that has already gone through is now in the past and the money has exchanged pockets and will be harder to keep track of.

Compliance: So there you have it. Compliance is simply making sure that we follow the rules, principles and laws surrounding accounting. While it is a simple topic, there is a lot to it. But as you've been reading through, I'm sure you'll notice how the average business that abides by the law isn't going to find it particularly difficult to keep compliant.

Chapter Summary

- There are two key frameworks for accounting: GAAP and IFRS. Both of these are different, with GAAP being much more rules-focused, but they both stress good accounting principles.

- Principles like the revenue recognition principles, the historical cost principle, the matching principle, the full disclosure principle, and the objectivity principle all keep modern-day accountants on the right side of the law and they reduce errors in reading reports.

- The revenue recognition principle is broken surprisingly often considering how easy it is. This principle states that you must record and recognize all your revenue as income. Basically, you can't take a tip without recording it for the books or you're breaking the law. This is an easy mistake to make but it is an extremely dangerous one because it can land you on the wrong side of the law quickly.

- The historical cost principle tells us that we must keep the costs of our assets as they were when purchased. Rather than changing the price of an asset because it has changed since acquisition, you must keep with the historical price. This keeps your records reflecting the money actually spent rather than altering it.

- The matching principle tells us that expenses from revenue must be accounted for in the same period as that revenue even if they weren't paid out yet. If you pay a commission to your employees on sales accounted for in July but don't pay it until August, you would still have to recognise that expense as part of that income even though the money doesn't leave hands yet. It was earned or incurred at the time of the revenue.

- The full disclosure principle states that we will be completely honest with our financial reports, we won't hide any information and we won't try to disguise any information. To put it bluntly, this principle states thou shall not lie on financial statements.

- The objectivity principle reminds us that the information we are sharing is neutral. It is not for us to create a narrative for investors. We aren't telling a story when we are making up our financial statements, we are just reporting the facts as reflected in the balance sheet, the income statement, the cash flow statement, and the statement of retained earnings.

- GAAP stands for Generally Accepted Accounting Principles. These principles are covered in the Federal Accounting Standards Advisory Board's handbook on accounting standards which can be found online at fasb.gov/accounting-standards.

- The GAAP has many, many rules and it is best to use the search function of your PDF reader or browser to search through it for issues related to your business frequently until you get a sense of it.

- Any American accountant should be familiar with the GAAP, which can make hiring a professional accountant an attractive idea.

- IFRS stands for International Financial Reporting Standards. The IFRS is used in most countries while America uses the GAAP.

- The IFRS are much less rule-based than the GAAP and instead they focus on teaching good principles.

- If you are American then you will only need to worry about the GAAP. However, browsing the IFRS can give you an idea of how the rest of the world manages their financial information and this can make you a better investor on the international scale.

- In accounting we must make sure that we comply with the laws and standards as set out by the various governmental bodies.

- The early-2000s saw the Sarbanes-Oxley Act come into effect after some major companies made international headlines for their accounting scandals. This act had eleven titles which together make the rules and regulations around accounting more clear. At the same time the act also increased the penalties for lying and trying to hide money and forging phony financial statements.

In the next chapter you will learn all about financial statements. From the balance sheet to the income statement and from the cash flow statement to the statement of retaining earnings, we'll be looking in depth at the various financial statements that accountants put together in order to maintain compliance and analyze how your company is doing.

CHAPTER FOUR

FINANCIAL STATEMENTS

Financial statements are confusing. Trust me when I tell you that I get it. Learning how to read and use them isn't exactly rocket science but it sure is boring. At least rocket science has, you know, rockets. Financial statements are just numbers and data, not really the type of thing to get excited about.

But they're incredibly important for every business, so we need to set aside our boredom and frustration and figure them out. Once you have you will find that financial statements aren't nearly as intimidating, or even as boring, as they seemed at first.

In this chapter we are going to aim to do just that. We'll start by first going over some key concepts that will make it easier to read, understand, and benefit from financial statements. Following that we're going to move into discussions about the various financial statements themselves such as the balance sheet, income statements, cash flow statements, and statement of retaining earnings. This chapter will thus serve as our first deep dive into the statements themselves. As these statements are the main bread-and-butter of accounting, it is important to pay attention and make sure that you grasp the information ahead.

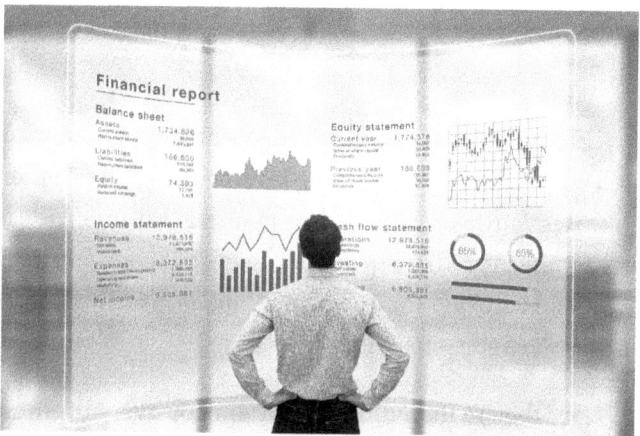

Understanding Financial Statements

Before we look at individual financial statements, it serves us best to look at financial statements as a whole. By approaching them in this manner we can create a framework through which to view them that we can return to whenever we get lost in the numbers and lose sight of our foundation. The key sections of financial statements are the balance sheet, the income statement, and the cash flow statement. Also extremely important are any notes you use to explain what investors are looking at when they consider your statements.

The first thing to understand about financial statements, far before you consider any particular component of them, is their purpose. Financial statements don't particularly make it any easier to run a company. If they are used properly then they can, but if you're dealing with things on a day-to-day basis and keeping tracking of things your own way then nothing is to say the business won't work. Financial statements aren't really for you so much as they are for others. Compliance is important but we're not talking about the government's need for your financial statements. No, instead it is better to consider your investors.

There are limitless investors out there and one or some of them may think that your company is a great idea and they may even consider investing in you. If they do then they are going to want to be able to see that their investment is paying off. Investors want to make sure that they are winning at this game, not losing. To that end, financial statements serve as scorecards that let investors know if they're making points or losing them. What framework an investor uses will determine how they interpret the data but that is an individual thing. In order to have this data they need the scorecard, i.e. your financial statements. Proper financial statements will show exactly where your company's numbers are.

In order to achieve this effect we use the balance sheet, the income statement, and the cash flow statement when performing investment analysis. There might be other tools that people want to see used but these are the key. Of these it is the balance sheet and the income statement that are most often used when making decisions but all three of these statements should be included together. The numbers in these statements represent financial information about how much is being made and how much is being spent, as well as information on the products and services and events that the company deals with or is affected by. These numbers are gathered by sticking to an established framework such as the GAAP so that everyone will be speaking the same language for better transparency.

One thing that we can figure out with a quick look at our financial statements is that they aren't the same. The GAAP helps to keep everything looking similar, in the same mold, but the information that is going to be in one company's financial statements is going to look different from the information in another company's. Business doesn't have a typical appearance. Rather, the world of business has a whole range of possibilities and each one is going to have different needs and they are going to handle them in different ways. This creates a diverse range of information that you could encounter in a financial statement. Don't look for a "standard" balance sheet that you can just copy. You must use your knowledge and experience to put together your own based on the unique circumstances of your company. As a quick addendum to that idea, consider spending some time reading up on financial terms and phrases. It can make it much easier to understand what you are doing or what you are seeing if you speak the lingo.

These statements are thus tools with a specific purpose and a specific way through which they are to be used. If you can wrap your head around them one at a time then you will be able to master the basic accounting skills you need to keep your business running legally, at least until it grows to the point where you need a dedicated accountant.

Balance Sheet

Your company's balance sheet is one of the financial statements which we generate through accounting. They cover a specific period of time and are used to help judge the capital structure of your business or to figure out what your rate of return is. It basically serves as a quick photo of where your company is at a particular point in time in relation to how much the company owes and how much it controls.

We use a simple formula when working on the balance sheet. Assets equal liabilities plus shareholders' equity. This basically means that the company must pay for the things it owns. This money can come from liabilities, such as borrowing money in the form of loans, or from shareholders' equity, i.e. using money provided by investors. If you take a $100 loan then you would have $100 in your assets and $100 in liabilities. If you take $100 from investors then your assets go up by $100 while the shareholders' equity also goes up by $100. When a company earns more money than it has expenses then it is placed in the shareholders' equity category. This is balanced on the assets side in different ways such as cash or company investments or new inventory. The fact that there can be different options for accounting for this new asset is made possible because assets, liabilities, and shareholders' equity all have different sub-categories in which you can note your resources.

Since the balance sheet is simply capturing what is happening with your company's finances at any given moment, it is most valuable when it is compared to balance sheets from earlier periods. Your company also exists within an industry that has competitors you should be following closely. Comparing your balance sheet against theirs can help you to get different ideas on how to run your finances. We talked about assets, liabilities, and shareholders' equity in chapter two but let us touch on them again briefly since these are the three components on the balance sheet.

Your assets are those items that can be turned into cash quickly. Assets include cash or any cash equivalents such as treasury bills. Marketable securities fall under assets, as well as your accounts receivable, your inventory, and any prepaid expenses the company has currently. These are all short-term assets because of how easily they convert to money. Long-term assets include things such as fixed assets like land or machinery, long-term investments, and intangible assets like the favors you are owed or any intellectual property you own.

Liabilities are money that you owe to others. These include short-term accounts such as what debt you have currently, how much you are indebted to the bank, how much interest you owe, your employee's wages or customers prepayments that need to be honored, any dividends you need to pay investors, the premiums that have been earned or that are soon to be, and, finally, your accounts payable. You also have long-term liabilities such as your long-term debt, pension fund liability, and deferred tax liability.

Shareholders' equity is the money that comes from your shareholders. Your retained earnings are added to the shareholders' equity because the shareholders' equity counts as the assets that your company has when liabilities are accounted for. Retained earnings can be used to pay off debts and the remaining money is shared with shareholders as dividends. A company can repurchase shares from shareholders to keep as treasury stock. Shareholders' equity isn't divided into short-term and long-term categories the way assets or liabilities are.

Your balance sheet will start with assets, list all the relevant categories, and come up with a total. It will then list the liabilities and go through the same, followed by the equity. You start at the top of the balance sheet and just read down in a straightforward manner. However, the balance sheet does have its limitations. For one, it only represents a single moment in time. It isn't particularly helpful for getting a sense of how a company has grown over time. As a document on its own there are a lot of ways that someone can read this. The best way to use balance sheets is to compare them and get that sense of what happened over time. There is still room for personal interpretation when this is the case but not to nearly the same degree as alone.

Revenue:
Net sales....
Interest earned
Less: Costs and expenses:
Cost of goods sold
Selling expenses
General & administrative expenses
Interest expense
Purchase discou...
Income tax
Total c...
...t inco...
...share

For the Year Ended December 31
Income Statement

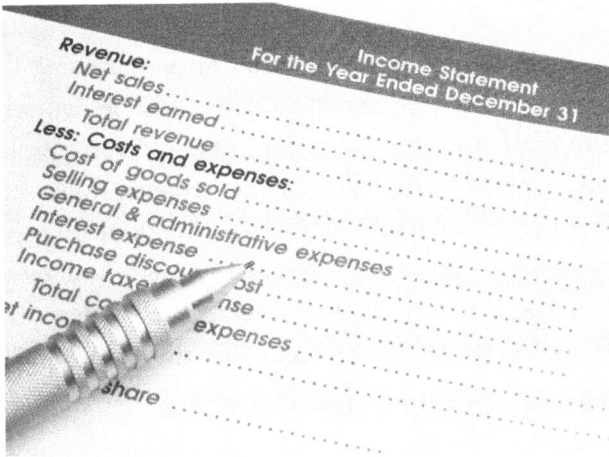

Income Statement

The income statement is sometimes referred to as the profit and loss statement or as the statement of revenue and expense. These alternative names, together with "income statement," really let you know that this statement is all about the money that is coming into and going out from your company. The goal of the income statement is to show your company's financial performance over a specific period of time. The income statement is a bit more complicated than the balance sheet, in my opinion, but it is just as important. We'll look through each of the sections, explore the structure and get a fully rounded grasp on these types of statements before moving onto our cash flow statements.

An income statement begins with a heading that specifies the accounting period it is concerned with. From there it breaks down into four sections: revenue, gains, expenses, and losses. These sections don't see a difference between sales in cash or sales done on credit. It starts with information related to sales and moves down the list until all four sections have been fully explored, at which point it then states the net income for the given period.

The first section is revenues but it is closely tied to the second section, gains, so as to make it most appropriate to look at the two sections together rather than one on one. We'll repeat this with the third and fourth sections for the same reason.

Revenues and gains are required to contain pretty much the same information no matter where you are from but how that information is formatted will be largely due to local restrictions and regulations. There are two types of revenue to be concerned with. The first is operating revenue and it is the revenue that comes from the main activities of your business. If you are in manufacturing then then the main activity would be the selling of goods and this would be where your operating revenue came from. If you are a company offering editing services to authors then your operating revenue would come from your services directly. This is in contrast to non-operating revenue which comes from secondary business activities. This revenue would be things such as rental income or revenue that was generated from interest, things like that. Gains are another form of revenue but one that comes from activities outside of the daily or typical processes of the company. If you were to sell long-term assets then the revenue that they generated would fall under the gains category.

One common problem that people face trying to figure out their income statements is that they confuse revenue with receipts. Revenue isn't directly tied to in-coming cash. Let's say you are putting together an income statement for one quarter. A week before that quarter ends a well-known client comes to you and purchases some goods. Since you know this customer well, you give them a month to make the payment. Their commitment to pay counts as revenue and it would be recorded as such. But it wouldn't be until they paid you the following month that you received the cash itself and thus generated a receipt. Some people get it in their head that they can't have revenue without a receipt but this mistake will result in your accounts being off.

Expenses are those costs that your business incurs while turning a profit. They are broken down into multiple subsections the same way that revenue is. Primary activity expenses are the expenses that you must pay in order to operate the business and earn your primary revenue. These include the costs of the goods you're selling or the cost of administrative expenses or research. Employee wages and sales commissions, even costs like electricity and gas all manage to fall under this category. Ultimately, most of your costs are likely to fall under primary activity. Secondary activity expenses are a much smaller category and they include costs that you pay onto business activities outside of your core. Costs such as interests on loans fall into this section. Losses are another form of expense but one in which the money spent is not going to be recouped. Losses include things like selling long-term assets at a loss or money spent settling lawsuits, basically anything where the money is lost and you won't see it again.

The primary revenue and primary expenses sections make up the core of your business. By looking at these two sections you can get a pretty great sense of how the company is performing in its duties. However, the secondary revenue and secondary expenses categories will give you a sense of how the company is running its other components. You could notice that there is a particularly large amount of secondary income and this could be a sign that the company needs to better manage its funds by investing further into areas like production or marketing or even straight-up expanding to sell a new product or offer a new service. Likewise, too many secondary expenses points towards a company that isn't managing its money so well or that is facing issues figuring out how to keep everything running as smoothly as possible. When reading an income statement, you want to make sure that you read and consider all the parts and not just those in the primary activities sections.

Income statements use these four sections (which in turn are made up of their own subsections) in order to generate a number for the company's net income during the period in question. You must first figure out those sections otherwise it will be impossible to complete the following mathematical formula. Once those section are figured out then the formula you apply to find your net income is:

Net Income = (Revenue + Gains) - (Expenses + Losses)

So let's see this in action using some simple numbers. Let's say you had revenue of $25,000 and gains of $1,000. But in the same period you had expenses of $12,500 and losses of $500. Now we can put this together to get:

Net Income = ($25,000 + $1,000) - ($12,500 + $500)

This in turn gives us:

Net Income = $26,000 - $13,000

And so we can easily solve this to get our net income:

Net Income = $13,000

This is one of those areas in accounting which is easy once you see it broken down but which can be quite complicated when first figuring it out on your own. This is one of those reasons why I always recommend that those who are new to accounting take the time to work through each of their statements at least twice. I want to be clear with this statement: I give you permission to mess up, but you must go through and check your numbers a second time to fix that mess up. If you don't then you will have issues. If you go through twice while still learning then you get more experience filling out your financial statements and you can catch those mistakes before they get sent off.

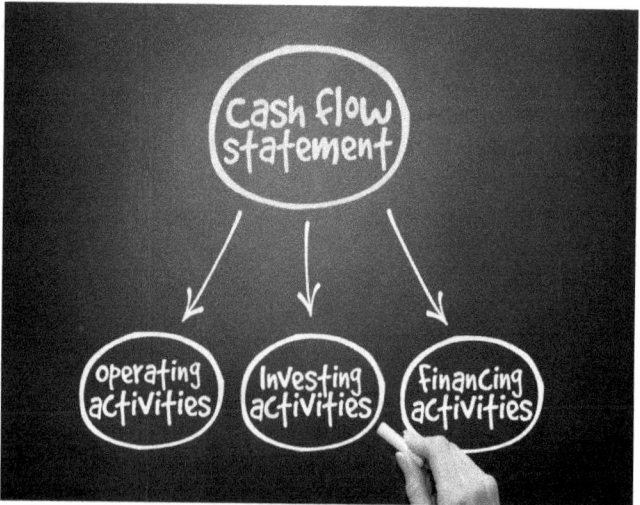

Cash Flow Statement

The cash flow statement's purpose is to summarize how much cash (or cash equivalents) have entered and left the company during the period in question. It, together with the balance sheet and the income statement, completes the financial statements which you are required by law to report. Investors use the cash flow statement to get an understanding of how the company is running, how it is making money, and how it is spending said money. Together with the income statement and the balance sheet, the cash flow statement allows investors to get an unbiased idea of how the company is doing so that they know, without a doubt, that they are happy with investing their money into the company.

A cash flow statement is structured into pieces the same way as any of these financial statements are. As each statement is composed of separate parts, they can be thought of as the sum of their parts and each section can be learned independently before being brought together in the whole. With the cash flow statement, those parts are the cash that comes from operating activities, the cash from investing, the cash from financing, and a disclosure of any noncash activities (which isn't always necessary but those following GAAP need to be sure to look into when it *must* be included). The cash flow statement does not make reference to credit, as the other statements have, but instead focuses exclusively on cash and not on net income. The most confusing of the sections is the cash from operating activities section and so we'll be exploring this first.

Operating activities, in regards to the cash flow statement, are those activities which actually use cash. This shows us how much cash the company has generated through their activities and it would include items like receipts from sales, receipts from services, payments made on interest or income tax, payments made to supplies or wage payments made to employees, payments made on rent, and anything else that could fall under operating expenses (this category can be extremely wide depending on the type of business such as how investment companies include debt and equity instruments). How these come together in calculating cash flow is a bit difficult. There are certain adjustments which are made to net income in order to calculate the cash flow. There are non-cash items that are calculated into a company's net income so these adjustments serve to remove these from the equation so that the cash flow statement focuses entirely on cash. To calculate your cash flow, you need to use either the direct cash flow or the indirect cash flow method.

The direct cash flow method is the easier of the two. It calculates the sum of the cash payments and receipts that the company has. These could include things such as cash that has been paid toward supplies or cash receipts from customers purchasing the company's services and cash that has been paid out to employees as wages. To figure out the sum of all these cash transactions the accountant uses the financial figures from the beginning of the period in question and compares it to the figures from the end of the period. They must look at all of the different business accounts rather than a singular one, of course, but this allows them to see what the net difference is. This net difference could be a positive one or a negative one.

The indirect cash flow method requires the accountant to first check the income statement in order to get the figure for the company's net income. The income statement is calculated and prepared using the accrual basis rather than purely focusing on cash. Remember how we prepared our income statements by noting the money we expected to come in when that customer of ours was given thirty days to pay? This is accrual accounting. We made note of that income when we made the transaction and earned it but not necessarily when it was paid to us. This means that the net income from the income statement is not the same as net cash flow and so we can't just use this number. The accountant needs to make adjustments to the figure from the income statement to figure out the cash flow.

As the accounts receivable on the balance sheet changes in a period, this is shown in the cash flow. If the number decrees on the balance sheet it means that there is more money coming into the company. Since more money has come in then we see the net sales increase by the amount the accounts receivable shrunk. When the number on the balance sheet increases, it means that the net sales see this amount taken away because that revenue is not cash but credit. When the inventory on the balance sheet increases then you need to check to see if it was bought with cash or with credit. If it was bought with cash then that increase on the balance sheet represents cash leaving the company and thus a smaller net sales number is generated. Purchases made on credit result in a higher accounts payable. If this number has changed for the better, the change increases the net sales. This process is added to other payable accounts such as insurance, salaries, or taxes payable. Basically, when something is paid off then we see that as cash leaving the company and a lower net sales but if it hasn't yet then we carry that difference forward as net earnings.

The investing activities part of the cash flow statement is calculated based on activities that change the company's overall assets, investments, or equipment. This section is most often a negative value because it is far more common for a company to purchase assets or equipment then it is for them to profit from selling them. It can happen, of course, but those are typically few and far between. The cash flow from financing activities part of the cash flow statement covers any cash coming or going from banks or investors, plus any cash that has been paid to shareholders in the form of dividends or buybacks. People reading a cash flow statement understand that a positive number represents raising money while a negative number indicates dividends or loans being paid.

Together these various categories will give the cash flow figure for the period in question. Most people automatically think that this number should be a positive, but a negative number isn't necessarily a bad sign. A negative number could be a bad sign but it could also mean that a company is expanding. This would naturally result in more money earned in the long run and thus make the company more attractive. Without further analysis, the negative number will seem quite unattractive. This is one reason why you should look at the financial statements for a company over multiple periods of time rather than just one individual period. It is also a reason why you should consult the balance sheet and the income statements that the company releases too. That way you can always get a full sense of what is happening.

Statement of Retained Earnings

Made in accordance with the GAAP, the statement of retained earnings shows the changes in a company's retained earnings over the period in question. This statement doesn't need to be a full document in the way that the others do, as it can be included on the balance sheet or on the income statement. This document tells the reader how the company's retained earnings has changed, what the net income for the period was, and how much the stockholders were paid in dividends. This will also have information on how the net income will be spent on certain things beyond the dividend payments to investors. We'll go over retained earnings again briefly to see how the statement of retained earnings benefits anyone reading the financial statements released for a given period of time.

Retained earnings come whenever your company makes money. This extra money is often used to make payments on debts or other financial obligations that the company has accumulated. If the company doesn't have any looming debts or is fine with them where they are then this money could be spent to grow the company. The money that a company has in retained earnings will be paid to investors and thus lower the overall amount of retained earnings that a company has. Money beyond what is paid out may be used to expand the company or create and market a new product, maybe it can be used for a merger or to buyback shares or pay off a loan. Pretty much any of the reasons that retained earnings are being spent are positive ones. Though it is best that they are being spent, as too many retained earnings over too long a period of time is a red-flag.

A statement of retained earnings is primarily designed to instill confidence in investors. It shows the investor how the retained earnings are being used to continue promoting company growth. The investor will be able to tell how much of their earnings the company is retaining. This is often called the retention ratio. This is simply how much much money the company is retaining for growth compared to how much they are paying out to investors. Investors see a company that is spending all of its earnings on outbound payments as risky. This tells them that the company might struggle to grow any larger. A company that keeps money for growth could be a sign of a good investment that will improve after purchase. Remember, however, that holding onto money for too long without reinvesting in the company is also a bad look. It's a bit hard to figure out how to walk the right way for investors but so long as you are committed to your company this shouldn't be a problem in the long run. Company growth is always attractive.

Chapter Summary

- Financial statements are one of the most important components of accounting simply due to the fact that you are legally required to provide them.

- Financial statements are generated and distributed in order to give investors a sense of where the company is. They allow an investor to see if they like the way the company is doing and they can decide if they want to stay on board with the company, buy more shares, or sell theirs based on the information in the financial statements.

- While financial statements are important, they aren't perfect documents. One investor can read one as positive while another reads it as negative. It depends on what standard the investor is looking to judge the company by.

- The numbers used in your financial statements must follow the GAAP. A benefit of this is that investors don't need to learn a unique system of accounting to see where you stand but rather they can easily and directly compare your company to any other.

- We use four financial statements to achieve this objective: the balance sheet, the income statement, the cash flow statement, and the statement of retained earnings.

- The balance sheet covers a specific period of time and shows a quick photo of where the company is at any one given time.

- The balance sheet is made up with the accounting equation of assets equal liabilities plus shareholders' equity.

- The balance sheet is best used when it can be compared to previous balance sheets that the company has generated. This allows investors to see how the company is functioning long-term rather than just a single image in time.

- Assets are items that can be turned into cash. Liabilities are money that you owe others and shareholders' equity is the money that comes from the shareholders and where your retained earnings reside.

- The balance sheet starts with assets and lists them all out in their different subcategories. Then it moves into liabilities and does the same before doing the same yet again with the equity. You can read a balance sheet from the top to the bottom to get a sense of how these different categories have shifted.

- The income statement is sometimes called the profit and loss statement. This statement shows a company's financial performance over a period of time.

- The income statement is broken down into revenue, gains, expenses, and losses.

- Revenue is the money that comes into your company through your main activities. Gains is money that comes into the company from activities beyond the scope of your typical business day such as when you sell long-term assets.

- Revenue is not the same as receipts. Receipts are directly tied to incoming cash. If you are owed $100 that you are expecting to get paid on Wednesday then that would still count as revenue because you already did the work and are owed that. It would not have a receipt yet and it wouldn't count as cash but it is revenue.

- Expenses are costs that a business incurs when making money. Having to pay employees or pay gas for transportation or purchase raw materials are all expenses. Losses are for expenses that incur outside of regular business activities such as when you sell long-term assets at a loss.

- Net income is figured out with the equation: **Net Income = (Revenue + Gains) - (Expenses + Losses)**.

- The cash flow statement tells the reader how much cash or cash equivalents the company has. This does not count money that is coming in at a later date the way that revenue does but rather it focuses on money that is in the form of cash only.

- Operating activities on a cash flow statement show activities which use cash and it shows how much has come in from things like sales or how much has left in the form of payments.

- The direct cash flow method calculates the sum of cash payments and receipts that the company has and uses the financial figures from earlier in the period to see what's changed.

- The indirect cash flow method requires the accountant to check the income statement to get the net income and then go through the documentation and numbers to remove anything that isn't cash and come up with an amount.

- The statement of retained earnings is made to the standards of the GAAP and it can be attached to a balance sheet or income statement.

This document tells the reader how much money you are holding onto.

- A company that doesn't hold onto any extra money is likely not going to grow much more and investing in them represents a riskier investment. A company that holds onto too much money also isn't showing confidence or skill in their ability to grow as a company.

- A good company saves up money to pay back equity or grow the company and so you can expect to see them holding onto money enough to get to a point where they can invest in their own growth.

In the next chapter you will learn about the point at which bookkeeping and accounting meet in the modern day. Recording transactions used to be the realm of bookkeeping but more and more accounting software has been taking over this responsibility and leaving it in the lap of accountants. We'll look at the general ledger, how trial balance is used, how we calculate for and record debits and credits, and how journal entries help us to achieve our accounting goals.

CHAPTER FIVE

RECORDING TRANSACTIONS

When people refer to bookkeeping a lot of the time what they mean is making sure the general ledger is up to date. This is the book where the financial records for the company are stored and it is directly involved in good accounting practices. Since bookkeeping and accounting are becoming more and more tightly woven together it is important for the accountant to understand how to record transactions and keep accurate records.

In this chapter we'll focus on doing just that. We'll start by looking at the general ledger and then move into a discussion on the role of trial balances. From there we'll discuss how we make use of debits and credits before we finish with a discussion on recording journal entries. Together these four sections will give you a quick but thorough understanding of how financial records and transactions are structured and stored for later use.

What is a General Ledger?

Back in the day, long before computers, transactions had to be written down in ink and kept up by hand. To keep all of these transactions in the same place, the general ledger was invented. This book let business owners keep track of their finances with ease. In order to keep them accurate and account for possible human error, the general ledger is kept using the double-entry method. This became less important as computers took care of things and made it easier but the general ledger has remained.

Most businesses use the double-entry accounting system, though they don't have to. You can personally use the single-entry accounting system if you really want to but it isn't recommended. The double-entry system is much better because it helps to increase the accuracy, but the general ledger for your company absolutely uses the double-entry system. This simply means that accounts are connected to each other so that an entry into the system in one account represents an opposite entry in a different account. Debits and credits balance each other out in this manner. We'll be looking at credits and debits shortly. We'll also be looking at journals, which are directly tied to the general ledger though they represent the step before data is recorded in the ledger.

Some companies don't use a general ledger but I want to recommend that you do, so let's get into those recommendations.

Why Use a General Ledger?

The most obvious reason for a general ledger is the fact that it lets you keep track of all your financial transactions. Using the general ledger will allow you to ensure that your financial transactions are recorded correctly and the double-entry system gives you extra comfort in knowing they're accurate.

A general ledger is useful in helping a business compile a trial balance, something that we'll be looking at in more detail in just a moment. Beyond that it also makes it easier to get your taxes done up since all of the information is kept in the same location. The less you need to go scrambling for a receipt at the last second, the easier your taxes will be. A general ledger is also good for getting a sense of how your company is managing its budget and you'll be able to get numbers on how much money you're spending and where so that you can adjust the budget with concrete numbers.

Another great thing about a general ledger is that it makes it easier to spot weird transactions and spot fraud. A lot of the time issues with fraud get by because there is not a system in place to spot it. Some cases can go years before getting caught simply because there weren't accurate records being kept of the company's financial records. Keeping a general ledger from the start is a good idea because it instills good healthy and honest record keeping and it makes it harder for fraud to happen and it gets a thousand times easier to spot when it does. Even if you can't prevent it, the sooner you spot it the sooner you can deal with it.

A general ledger isn't necessarily something that you might need for your company but it is one of those things that you can truly benefit from using anyway. As the company grows you'll find that it comes to be even more handy and it is always easier to learn how to use a general ledger in the beginning when things are slower than when things are zooming around you and you're trying to manage your employees, expand your business, and learn how to use a general ledger all at the same time.

What Is a Trial Balance and How Does It Play a Role in Accounting?

The trial balance has one of those names that can make you nervous. Don't worry, nobody is putting you on trial and this has nothing to do with breaking the law. Instead this is a trial in the sense that it is a short, quick, and easy way to see if your accounts are looking good without having to crunch all of the numbers at once.

A trial balance is done by taking the balances of all the accounts in your company's general ledger. Some accounts will have a balance of zero and these can be left out or included, they really won't make a difference in this particular exercise. Accounts are broken up into debit accounts and credit accounts and the amount from each account is placed into the appropriate section. After all the accounts have been divided into these two sections they are totalled. If things are going properly then the amount in the debit balances and the amount in the credit balances sections will be the same.

A trial balance is in no way a financial statement. Instead it is used for internal accounting and bookkeeping purposes to see if there is a problem somewhere. When the accounts don't line up in a trial balance then there could be an issue in what was reported, there could be a mistake in the account balances somewhere, or a credit might have been mislabelled as a debit, or the opposite may have happened. Most accounting software will spot these issues for you ahead of time and this makes the trial balance exercise less useful, but if you are working by hand then checking the trial balance will be more important and you should make running a trial balance a weekly or even a daily goal depending on how much business your company sees.

Understanding Debits and Credits

Debits and credits are one of the more confusing areas of accounting but they are the cornerstone of the double-entry system. I believe that the reason people have such trouble with debits and credits is not because of how they function but rather the names they have been given. Debit brings to mind debit cards and credit brings to mind credit cards and customer credit, but they mean different things when it comes to keeping track of financial transactions.

The easiest way to break down debits and credits is:

Debits represent money flowing in.

Credits represent money flowing out.

Debits are on the left. Credits are on the right.

To understand this in action, let's look at an example. Your company is broken up into all sorts of different accounts. You earn money working for the day and you put the cash you earned into the cash account. This would be a debit of the amount equal to how much you put into the cash account. If you take $1000 out of the cash account to purchase a new computer then this would be a credit of $1000 to the cash account because the money is coming out. But since the money is buying a computer, the computer is an asset and that $1000 would be debited into the account relating to equipment. This means that the cost in cash was removed from the company but converted into the equivalent amount as an asset.

Keep in mind that not every account is a positive one. The accounts used to purchase the computer are accounts that track the assets the company has. There are accounts that are used for tracking the company's liabilities such as when you have an account for loans you've taken from the bank. When you are dealing with an account like this then you would debit your cash account for the amount you gained in the loan but you would also credit your loan account because it is a liability. It represents an amount you have to pay rather than the amount you have of something. We see this happen the same way when dealing with equity raised by investors. The cash section gets debited but the equity account is credited. Equity accounts go up when they are credited because they measure what investors have in your company rather than anything your company has itself.

Debits and credits can remain pretty difficult so try to keep these tips in mind.

1. Debits raise asset accounts but credits lower them.
2. Debits raise expense accounts but credits lower them.
3. Debits lower liability accounts but credits raise them.
4. Debits lower equity accounts but credits raise them.
5. Debits lower revenue but credit increases it.

6. Debits are always recorded on the left with credits recorded on the right.

Recording Journal Entries

Journal entries in accounting is more of a method of recording an accounting transaction than it is a way of leaving detailed notes like you might think of when you think of a personal journal. Regardless, a good accountant can read journal entries of this type with just as much clarity. Journal entries are often worked into the general ledger but they are sometimes divided into smaller ledgers that will then be added to the general ledger at a later date. These journal entries make the world of accounting much easier.

The journal entries used in accounting must be at least two lines long. They can be longer than this, as there is no limit to how many can be included so long as there are at least two at the beginning. A journal entry that has only two entries is a simple journal entry while those with more than two items are called compound journal entries. While it might seem natural to think that putting as much information onto an entry at a time would be the best approach this isn't always the case. Often it is actually easier to take about a particular piece of information when it stands on its own and can easily be referenced when it is needed.

So... what is a journal entry?

Simply put, a journal entry is the way that we record debits and credits. Those annoying things from just a minute ago? Yup, them. The reason that there has to be at least two lines to an entry is because you must balance out a debit with a credit. The amount of money in any journal entry, or transaction, must equal out when the debits and credits are compared to each other. If they don't equal out then your accounts aren't balanced and there is a problem somewhere.

A journal entry must show both of the accounts involved, the one getting the debit and the one getting the credit. The date must be recorded. You must also take note under which accounting period the entry is being made. A journal entry must have the name of the person making the entry. If the person making the entry is not a manager then it must have a manager's signature. The journal entry must be given a number for further reference. It must be noted whether or not the entry is a one time thing or if it is a repeating entry and any documentation related to the entry should be included. At the very least a journal entry should have a short paragraph, even just a couple of sentences, about what the journal entry represents.

While this is what your journal entries must have at a minimum, there are different types of journal entries. The common journal entry is a one time entry and it can be noted fairly easily. A reversing journal entry is one that is reversed, as the name implies. A recurring journal entry is one that will recur in multiple accounting periods and it typically needs to be given a termination date in order to finish.

These tools are easy to use, simply record the debits on the left and the credits on the right and always make sure there are at least two sections. It is easiest to write down the list of requirements for a journal entry and keep them on a sticky note for quick reference. They're not so much complicated as they are tedious to remember so keeping them near at hand will make recording your journal entries that much easier.

Chapter Summary

- Recording transactions is technically the realm of bookkeeping but it is important for accountants to learn as these two roles become more closely related.

- A general ledger is a book which keeps track of all the financial transactions for a company. The general ledger may have all of the accounts listed in it or it may have sections of the company's accounts broken down into smaller ledgers which themselves are stored within the general ledger.

- The general ledger keeps all of the financial information in one location so that it is easy to reference it as it is needed for accounting purposes.

- A general ledger requires the double-entry accounting system in order to function. This means that when an entry is made in an account, there is another equal entry in a related account. By using the double-entry accounting system it is easier to keep everything balanced and in order.

- The general ledger allows you to compile a trial balance.

- One of the best aspects of a general ledger is the way that it lets you catch weird transactions early and spot fraud. By being aware of financial transactions as they happen it is easier to catch the weird ones while there are still options for how to deal with them.

- You might think that there is no value to using a general ledger in your company if it is quite small but the sooner you do, the better it is. Getting used to working with a general ledger can get you and your managers thinking about finances earlier and this is always a positive for a business.

- A trial balance is a way of quickly seeing if your accounts are balanced without having to do any heavy lifting. A trial balance takes all of the company's accounts and divides them into debit accounts or credit accounts. Each category gets totalled together and it is expected that credit and debit accounts will equal each other out. If they don't then there is a problem that must be fixed.

- A trial balance is not a financial statement. Instead it should be considered as a quick tool for checking if the accounts are balanced. Beyond this it doesn't offer much value in the long-run. Rather, it is a way to save yourself some work. If everything is balanced then the

111

ACCOUNTING

accountant can rest easy. If it isn't then there is work to be done and a problem to solve.

- Debits and credits are confusing in accounting because they don't have anything to do with debit or credit as it is typically thought of.

- Debits in accounting represent money flowing into an account.

- To credit an account represents money that is flowing out.

- Debits and credits are listed in the general ledger. Debits are always on the left and credits are always on the right.

- Debits raise asset accounts and expense accounts. Credits lower asset accounts and expense accounts.

- Debits lower liability accounts and equity accounts. Credits raise liability accounts and equity accounts.

- Debits lower revenue, credit raises revenue.

- Not every account is a positive one. Some accounts are increased by crediting such as accounts that represent equity. Taking out more money debits the account it moves the money into and it credits the account representing loans (or however the money was generated). Because the higher a number in an equity account, the more that is owed, a credit to this account represents an increase in the amount owed. A credit represents money leaving an account but so does this account. The higher the number in the account, the more money you owe and thus the more money that is ultimately leaving in tune to the transaction.

- Journal entries are a way of recording an accounting transaction in the general ledger. A journal entry must be at least two lines long. The first line records the debit, the second line records the credit. Two lines is the minimum it takes to properly record a journal entry for a double-entry system.

- A journal entry can be as long as you want it to be but it is better to record multiple short entries than to record one long entry. Since each entry is given a unique number for later reference, it is easier to find the information you need when it is labelled on its own rather than as part of something larger.

- Each journal entry must show the accounts involved, the date it is recorded, the accounting period it is for, the name of the person making the entry, the manager's signature, a unique number for later reference, a note on whether the entry is one time or recurring, and any additional documentation that is necessary for record keeping purposes.

- A one-time entry is the most common. A recurring journal entry is one that repeats in later accounting periods and typically it must be stopped manually or it will continue to recur. A reversing journal entry is one that is reversed and thus is used for fixing errors and the like.

In the next chapter you will learn about managerial accounting. You've already seen that this type of accounting is used to generate reports that are used internally rather than externally but it's now time to put these ideas into action in order to create budgets, run margin analyses and cash flow analyses, forecast your findings, and calculate your financial leverage.

CHAPTER SIX

MANAGERIAL ACCOUNTING

For our last chapter in this introduction to accounting we are going to look at managerial accounting. This form of accounting, as discussed in chapter one, is entirely focused on generating reports and data that help with the internal running of the company. The reports that we make in managerial accounting are not intended to be read by anyone outside of the company and there is no one right or wrong way to generate them. If you make a mistake in your managerial accounting then you are going to have a rough time trying to run the company off faulty data but you aren't going to end up on the wrong side of the law.

With that said, we must make note of the importance of keeping our managerial accounting in line with itself. If we decide to make use of managerial accounting then we must create guidelines to follow that keeps all of our financial data looking the same. Financial accounting has the GAAP and IFRS to keep it in line but these can be thrown out the window for managerial accounting. But just because they can doesn't mean that they should. It is better to stick with the principles that your company uses in their financial accounting. Doing so will ensure that your internal reports can be read and compared to your external reports. This isn't important for investors or anything but it can help to provide your managers and yourself with as much data as possible.

I am of the mindset that when it comes to running your business, data is the most important thing in the world. The more data you can have, the better you can understand the situation you find yourself in at any given moment. I also believe that to keep up with all of your financial data on a regular basis is a great way to spot fraud or errors early and prevent them from causing long-term damage, which happens when a small error goes unnoticed and is allowed to snowball and grow larger each new reporting period.

This chapter focuses on those managerial accounting tools that all beginners need to learn. They include the basics like budgeting and forecasting, margin analysis and cash flow analysis, and a look at financial leverage. Once you have a solid grasp of these skills you will be ready to start applying them to your company to see how they work in action to give you more knowledge and a better understanding of your company's accounting.

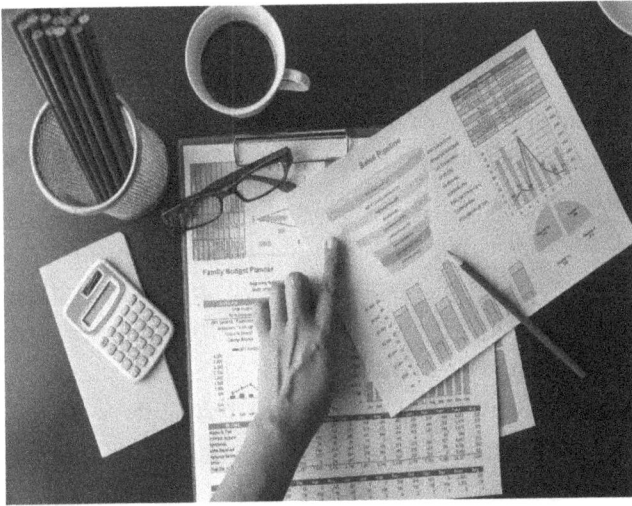

Budgeting

Budgets are one of the most important tools that your company's managers can have. Most people think they understand what a budget is but there are actually a few different types that we'll be looking at. Before we get into types, let's just set down a basic definition to begin with. A budget, in managerial accounting, is any document which sets out goals for the use of finances during a given period of time. That period of time could be a day, a week, a month, a quarter, a year, or more. The when of it is less important than the concept that a budget is a guideline for how to spend money.

There are many reasons that your company should use a budget. In fact, there are many reasons why each and every person reading this should have a budget, even just a personal one. We'll stick to the benefits that they provide to your company in this book. One of the biggest things a budget does for a company is give the management of the company the ability to look ahead and make goals and plans. A budget gives you a sense of where the money is going at any given time, or rather it gives you a sense of where the money is supposed to go. Just because we make a budget doesn't mean that we are going to follow it. We are supposed to but it is very easy to make mistakes and spend where we aren't supposed to. If we make a budget then the idea inherent in that is that we are going to stick to it. If we do stick to it like we are supposed to then we absolutely can use a budget to give a sense of where our finances are going to be in the future and we can make plans for how to use them. A budget makes growing your company easier.

A budget also helps managers to get the company's spending under control and to be more involved in each part of the company. For example, you might have managers that spend all of their time out on the floor looking over the employees and convincing customers to purchase goods. Meanwhile the shipping department is being run pretty much manager-free. The manager might have no idea how much money is actually being used by the department. Once you have a budget in place, the department knows exactly how much money they have to spend and if they need more then they will have to come talk to someone about it. Rather than money simply leaving the company, the budget helps to put limits on the amount and foster discussion between the various departments of the company. As discussions between the various departments take off it helps to create a sense of togetherness through the company rather than creating bubbles of isolation.

Budgets are also useful in getting your managers more into the mindset of the accountant. While you don't necessarily want your managers to be accountants themselves, you do want them to be aware of the reality of financial transactions, keeping good records, and considering the company's finances before making decisions. These are all good practices for your managers to be accustomed with. The more your managers understand the financial side of the company, the better they get at working with the company that way. Even more important is that a financially educated manager is a manager who is much more likely to spot some kind of fraud or issue. The perfect company would never deal with fraud or financial problems but this is simply an unrealistic standard to try to live by. Instead it is best to teach your managers so that their eyes become watchful for the signs of problems in their early stages.

There are several types of budgets and it can be valuable to see the differences between them. Many people think of a budget as being a singular thing but it all depends on how it is built.

A master budget falls in line with what people typically think of when they hear the word. This is a budget that projects how each and every aspect of the business is going to run over the period of the budget. Most of the time a master budget is made for a period of a year but this isn't always the case. A new company might find it more valuable to create a master budget on a quarterly basis, as the company could easily fold before the end of a year if it isn't careful. A master budget creates a cash budget, an income statement, and a balance sheet that has been budgeted. A lot of the time a master budget can be composed of smaller budgets from each of the different departments within the company. By connecting smaller budgets into the master budget it helps to keep each department on the same page. That said, this is definitely an approach favored more by larger companies than smaller ones.

A cash flow budget is one that looks at how cash flows into and out of the business daily. This budget is used to predict how much money the company will make with the goal of showing that the company makes more than it loses. Managers can use this to get a sense of how the income is doing compared to costs like production. It also gives managers a sense of when the inventory needs to be restocked.

An operational budget that covers revenue and expenses is a daily budget that focuses on the company's primary business. Operating budgets like this are made for a year or a larger period of time and then broken down into shorter periods. Managers are able to use the operation budget that covers revenue and expenses similarly to the cash flow budget, but it has a wider net for the data it concerns itself with.

These are just a few of the types of budgets that a company may want to make up. There are lots of other types of budgets but they push beyond the realm of the beginner accountant and start to get into much more complex territory. It is important to remember for the time being that your company will benefit from a budget. You might want to simple set limitations around spending or you may want to get more involved and run multiple types of budgets. You don't need to jump off into the deep end right away but you should begin using budgets as early as possible for the best results and the highest level of control over your company's finances.

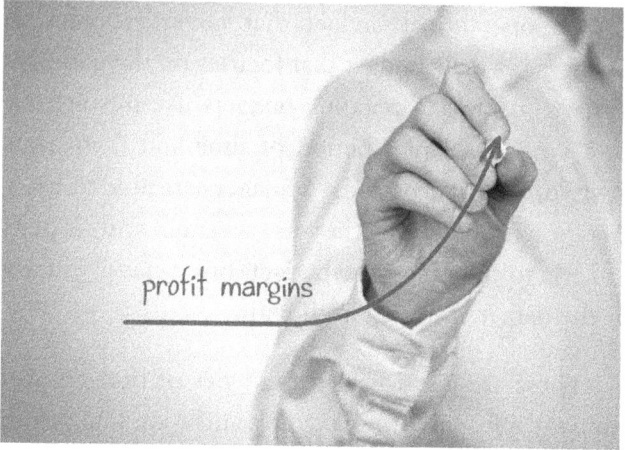

profit margins

Marginal Analysis

Marginal analysis is a bit of a tricky one. It is the name we give to the examination of the benefits of an activity compared to the additional costs of that activity. These benefits can be wide-ranging, as many activities aren't particularly useful for generating cash. For example, marketing your product with an Instagram influencer doesn't directly bring you back money but the promotion is a benefit for your company that must be considered. Marginal analysis is most often used in determining hiring decisions or product production decisions such as "Does hiring another worker make us back more money than we spend paying them?" or "Does it make more sense to order 10 copies of this product or 20? 50? 100?" These are cases where marginal analysis is used to figure out the answer.

The idea behind marginal analysis is that small changes have big effects. We've discussed this idea again and again from a negative perspective such as when we make mistakes in our bookkeeping and it comes back to haunt us. Marginal analysis is a way of testing out these small changes in a neutral setting. The idea here is that each part of the company is just part of a larger system. This system often consists of systems within systems such as when you have multiple departments in the company. When you want to make a change in any one part of the system there is going to be a ripple effect that changes the rest of the system. This ripple can be for the best or for the worse but regardless of which it still happens. Rather than simply introduce the change into the system as it is, marginal analysis gives us a way of testing out this change to see what happens before we commit to it.

Marginal analysis weighs the costs and the benefits of the change to see what happens. Sometimes a change seems necessary, such as hiring a new employee, but a marginal analysis reveals that the cost would be too high compared to the benefits. One place where marginal analysis really shines is where you are faced with more than one option you have to choose from. Let's say you can invest in one improvement to the company but that's all. Marginal analysis will help you to figure out which choice is going to be the most beneficial to the company as a whole. It is achieved easily enough; just take your current financial information and change the numbers to reflect the next situation you are considering. Increase the amount of money being spent and likewise increase the amount of inventory, employees, or whatever it is that you are increasing. This gives you new data that you can use in forecasting to see if the choice is the one that benefits the company the most. Remember to run marginal analysis for each of the options you are considering, not just one. It is only through multiple analyses that you can find the best solution.

Marginal analysis is only focused on a single change at a time. Because of this it can be easy to try out one change and see that it would have a positive impact. Seeing a positive impact, it would be easy to consider the day done early and just go with that one positive. But marginal analysis does not help you choose which options are better. It only allows you to highlight one change. While the first change you explore may be positive that doesn't mean that it is the best change. So, again, consider marginal analysis as a process in which you must go through all the choices you are weighing in order to find which one is the best.

Also remember that marginal analysis is not the end-all-be-all of managerial accounting techniques. It can be an extremely useful tool but it is not some powerful game changer. It comes from the economic theory of marginalism and this theory has been criticized in the past for being rather hard to contain. One of the things that marginalism requires is for the markets to be perfect and this just isn't how the world works. Markets are anything but perfect, especially these days. However, while marginalism isn't a perfect theory it does give us marginal analysis and this tool is powerful. You shouldn't purely rely on marginal analysis for making your decisions; after all, marginal analysis could reveal that the best choice is to let go of somebody or hire somebody new when you know that it isn't the right time. Marginal analysis should be considered a tool but it is still up to the administrative staff in the company to make the calls. Sometimes a gut feeling proves to be more valuable than all the hard data in the world or anything that comes up in a marginal analysis.

Being flexible is important. Make use of marginal analysis in your company but don't treat it like some oracle with all the answers. You're still the one who ultimately has to weigh the pros and cons of all the decisions made on behalf of the company.

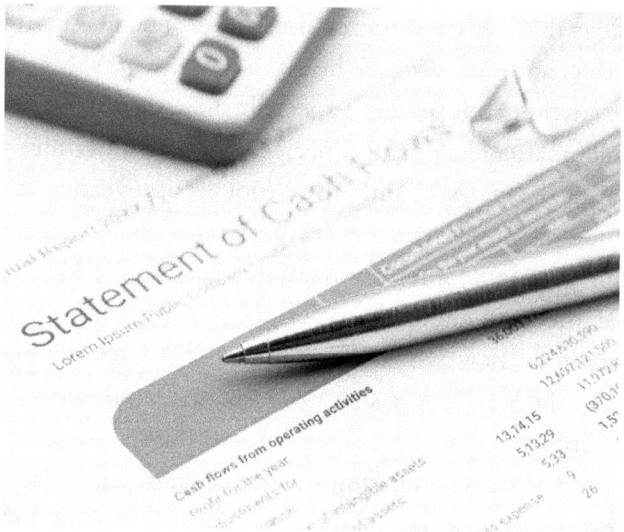

Cash Flow Analysis

Cash flow analysis is the analysis of the cash flow statement. This statement is one of the four key financial statements that we looked at in chapter four. In that chapter we looked at how the cash flow statement helps investors to see what is happening with the excess cash your company has generated. While you must learn to use the cash flow statement for external purposes, this is one of those documents which can be just as useful when used internally. One of the biggest issues that smaller companies face is running out of cash. When there's no money left it's awfully difficult to run a company. Performing regular cash flow analysis is a

126

good way to ensure that you are never caught unawares by a cash problem.

The cash flow statement is a financial statement which shows how money comes into and leaves your business during the period in question it represents. This document is extremely important, legally, but it is just as important for you. You may have to provide a cash flow statement for a given period of time but that doesn't mean it is the only one you have to generate. Generating cash flow statements at more regular intervals is always a smart idea.

A cash flow statement is already a smart choice to generate because it provides a snapshot of the way cash is flowing into or out of the company. This doesn't particularly help you out much if you can't analyze it. Cash flow analysis allows you to tell if your cash is looking good or not, if you will have problems making payments or not. By performing cash flow analysis you will be able to tell if you need to adjust your budget or make changes to your cash flow. If the analysis shows a shortage then you can plan for it, if it shows excess cash then you start to contemplate where it should be spent such as in the budget for new equipment or the like. Cash flow analysis performed on a regular basis is the secret weapon your business has so that it never finds itself unable to pay a bill or keep up with an expense.

Before you can analyze your cash flow you first need a cash flow statement. For more information on a cash flow statement, see chapter four. With the cash flow statement made you can then analyze it. This is easier than generating the cash flow statement in the first place. Start by looking at the cash flow from operations section of the cash flow statement. Your goal with the cash flow from operations section is to see the number increase as often as possible. If the number is staying the same or getting smaller then there is an issue with cash flow in your basic operations. Next you should identify how much of your revenue is still yet to be paid by customers. This gives you a sense of what cash you can expect to see coming shortly. Keep an eye on any cash that is being spent on new equipment or the like as this cash should be earned back in future statements because of the increased efficiency of the company due to the new acquisition.

As you move through your cash flow analysis, these are just a few of the areas that you will want to keep your eye on. What we are looking for with an analysis is to really see where the money is going and to spot patterns whenever possible. Humans are creatures of habit and patterns and this means we're actually really great at spotting them. If we're doing regular cash flow analyses then we will be able to see these patterns and learn from them. You could think that money is good until right around the time that the bills are due and this has caused issues. You could use this knowledge to change the way you are handling your money so that you aren't short when it comes to bills and you don't need to make late payments anymore. You could also see patterns that help to inform your decisions around staff payroll or overspending on inventory or when to make bill payments or how effective your marketing has been. You could learn more about when to raise your prices and when to stop extending credit to certain customers. There is a lot that you can learn from cash flow analysis.

So next time you generate a cash flow statement, take the time to break it down and really analyze it. Make this step a part of your regularly scheduled managerial accounting and you will find it proves to be beyond beneficial.

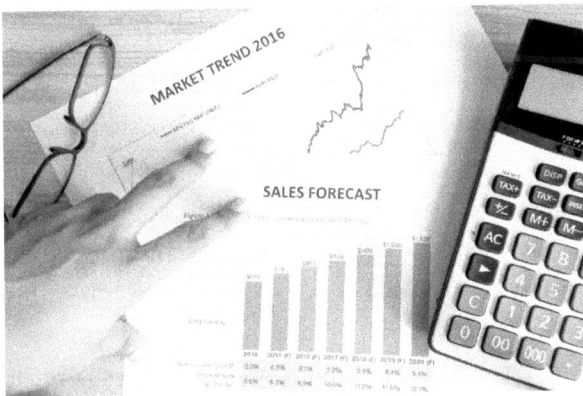

Forecasting

Forecasting is the process through which accountants use data about both current and historical costs in order to predict what something will cost in the future. Forecasting is important because it helps us to better plan our company's future by taking an educated guess as to how much it will cost to continue running primary operations. Forecasting allows us to better create our budgets and thus it has the added benefit of helping us to more fully and accurately make use of our other managerial accounting tools. Since we already looked at budgeting in this chapter we won't have a second discussion on it. Just know that budgeting is one of the tools that combines with forecasting in order to truly level up.

Another tool that forecasting gives us access to is called the high-low method. This method is used for estimating costs through forecasting. It is quite simple and this makes it easy to learn but that simplicity does come at a cost. Because the high-low method is simple, it necessarily isn't the most accurate approach we can use. The easier something is in accounting, the less information it is using. This is a rule of thumb and there are clear examples that break it but for the most part you can trust it. The key to understanding this result is simply to consider how complicated business truly is. As soon as you start to remove data, you start to lose accuracy. That doesn't make it useless. If you are looking to forecast quickly then the high-low method is the go-to approach.

Basically the high-low method uses extremes of data to forecast. You must have data about the costs and the cost-driver activities that are relevant to your company. The high-low method requires us to take the highest cost and the highest cost-driver activity level, as well as the lowest cost and lowest level of cost-driver activity. Once we have these pieces of data we can then use them to calculate what they would like graphed out and connected with a single line. We're interested in discovering what the slope of the line between them is. This slope and one of the four data points are used together to figure out where the intercept is located. Once it is found you have the information for the high-low cost equation of the activity that you are forecasting.

Another approach is called regression analysis. This form of analysis figures out how much variance in a dependent variable is due to the variations in an independent variable. This is a harder form of analysis that is best handled with technology rather than by hand. Regression analysis can be done for a single set of independent and dependent variables or it can be done across multiple. Regardless of how many variables there are in play, regression analysis requires data about both variables to be provided. The end result of regression analysis is an equation that is used in forecasting. This equation is used to help forecast costs based on the information revealed about the independent variable.

Basically, forecasting is a way of estimating data more accurately. You could assume that you understand how much it costs to run your business over a given period but those costs are prone to change as the world changes, as manufacturing changes. There is a whole world of change which comes together to affect the cost of maintaining your business. While forecasting does not allow us to overcome these changes, it is helpful. We can't forecast major world-changing events like a global pandemic or a recession but we can look at how prices have changed throughout our history with them and use this to predict how they will continue to change in the future.

Forecasting is not future-sight. There is no look into the future to see how it will play out. Rather, it is a way of future prediction; it predicts that things will continue to change in accordance to how they've already changed. By accounting for change in this manner we can get a better understanding of what is in store for our company and this allows us to more accurately budget for and react to changes as we face them. It doesn't prepare us for the extraordinary but it does prepare us for the predictable aspects of the future.

Financial Leverage

Financial leverage is the name we give to the practice of using debt to purchase assets. We use financial leverage to increase how much we make from equity. For example, an investor gives $100 to the company. In order to leverage that money you use the $100 to purchase a new printer that allows you to print out merchandise at twice the speed you could previously. Now that $100 will be able to make you back much more than $100 and it means you have a larger return on equity thanks to it. The problem with this approach is that to stretch yourself out too far with too much financial leverage is not a good thing and it can often be a sign that a company is going to fail in the future. Too much leverage makes it harder to repay the core debt and this can signal failure.

Financial leverage is determined by a ratio that compares total debt to total assets. The amount of debt to assets increases in tune with the amount of financial leverage your company is said to have. It is no surprise that the best use of financial leverage is when you are sure that the use will generate back more revenue than the debt you've incurred to spend on it. Financial leverage has an advantage over raising more equity capital because it doesn't lower the earnings per share of the shares that stockholders' already own. Financial leverage can make it so that your company earns more on assets or it can increase the amount of interest you have on your equity and this is sometimes of benefit for reducing your company's taxable income so that you can land in a cheaper tax bracket.

Although financial leverage can help you to earn back a disproportionate amount, it can also cause you to lose this as well. It is important that you consider fully how much interest you will have to expend thanks to financial leverage. You shouldn't use financial leverage on any projects or purchases that aren't going to increase your earnings enough to cover the higher interest rate. It is also important to consider how financial leverage can affect the investors looking at your company. Financial leverage often results in large changes in a company's profits and this can make the price of company shares less organized. Stocks that are more volatile are often more valuable and so this can be a good thing but it can cause issues such as when shares are issued to company employees.

Financial leverage can be a risky way to approach your business. Figuring out when you want to make use of financial leverage and when it is best avoided can be hard to do. There tends to be a limit of financial leverage. There isn't any set rule or anything like that but rather financial leverage requires equity and those that lend money are naturally less likely to lend money to someone that already owes a lot.

Financial leverage is a way that allows a company to use the debt it has acquired to earn more money but it is a risky maneuver because by design it requires the company to increase its debt. If you don't increase your debt, you can't leverage it financially. The safest bet is always to ensure that the money you are using to purchase assets is money that the company is making rather than money it has to borrow.

Business isn't always about taking the safest route. Sometimes you need to take risks, that's just the way it is. But you shouldn't take risks without first being prepared. Before you start making plans for leveraging your finances, take a moment to create a budget, run some margin analysis. Take the time to estimate whether or not the path in front of you is the most beneficial for your company. At the very least you must figure out how badly you will be impacted by the higher interest if your plan to earn enhanced revenue fails. If you can't survive your plan failing then you shouldn't bother with financial leverage. It is too risky.

If you can survive your plan failing, then give it a try. Your goal is never to have the plan fail, so hopefully it won't even matter. You want to ensure that it can before you go ahead, however. As long as it can, you don't need to worry about the company failing beneath you because of poor financial leveraging decisions.

Chapter Summary

- Managerial accounting is the type of accounting that focuses on generating financial information for use within the company. Managers make use of the reports generated through managerial accounting to make accurate and informed decisions about the company's finances.

- Managerial accounting does not need to stick to the GAAP or IFRS the same way that financial accounting does. Since the reports that managerial accounting generate are for internal use, there is no template that must be followed for legal purposes.

- Budgeting is a practice that is beneficial on the personal level but your company absolutely should be making use of budgets. Budgets are simple guidelines for how the company should be and plans to spend its money. A budget helps to reduce overspending.

- A company benefits from a budget for the reduction in overspending but also by the way it gives the reader a clear view of how the company is spending its money. A budget is also useful for connecting various departments together. A manager might not have much reason to speak to a particular department but if there is a budget in place then that department must get authorization for further spending and this can foster clear communication throughout the company.

- Budgets also help to get managers thinking more like accountants and really considering the financial realm. A good manager should be able to balance finances in their head but a well-structured budget will make the task even easier.

- There are different kinds of budgets such as master budgets, cash flow budgets, and operational budgets. Figuring out which type of budget your company should be using depends on the size, goals, and industry that the company exists within.

- Marginal analysis is an examination of the costs and benefits associated with any activity within the company. This is most often undertaken when considering how much product to produce or whether or not you should hire a new employee.

- Marginal analysis is the process through which we compare how much something costs to how much it is expected to help us. If we are increasing costs then we must also increase how much money we are making. Marginal analysis is one of the tools we use to achieve this.

- Marginal analysis believes that small changes have big effects. This means that a small change, such as hiring a new employee, has a big effect on how the future plays out. Marginal analysis basically estimates how the future would look if the company were to make one small change. This change is then calculated for and financial statements are generated to give an idea of how it will affect the company in the long run.

- Because marginal analysis is only focused on a single change at a time, you will find that you have to run several in order to weigh your options at any given time. If you have three options for how to act, marginal analysis must be run on each.

- When marginal analysis is run on one item, it may show that item would have a positive change on the company. Before you go ahead and implement that change, make sure to run marginal analysis on the other options. It could just be that another option has an even more positive effect.

- Cash flow analysis is the process of analyzing a cash flow statement. Cash flow statements show how much cash a company is dealing with but it merely serves as a snapshot of a moment in time. In order to truly benefit from this statement, you must perform analysis on it.

- Cash flow analysis is undertaken in order to see if you are making as much money as you should be. One of the biggest challenges that newer businesses face is to keep enough cash around to pay for the bills and keep the lights on. A cash flow statement shows you where your cash flow has been but a cash flow analysis is the process through which you read that data and come to an understanding of how it is functioning in the long term.

- Forecasting is the process through which accountants use data about the current and historical costs of production in order to predict the future cost. By using historical data an accountant is able to see how the price has changed between the historical figure and the current one. This change then lets the accountant forecast forward to predict how the price will continue to change in the future.

- Forecasting is not an exact science. Forecasting can never account for the weirdness of life like recessions or pandemics. Because of this it is important to keep in mind that a forecast is a prediction and not a guarantee. You can predict where the price will be but only time will tell you if that prediction was right or not.

- Forecasting can use the high-low method, in which the highest cost and highest cost-driver activity level is compared against the lowest cost and lowest level of cost-driver activity in order to make a prediction.

- Another approach is regression analysis which uses an independent and a dependent variable in order to forecast predictions.

- Financial leverage is using debt in order to purchase assets. Basically, it is using that new bank loan to purchase assets that will generate income for the company.

- Financial leverage can lead to enhanced earnings but it is also a riskier investment because you need to accrue debt to use. It isn't rare for a company to have too much financial leverage and be unable to pay the interest on it.

FINAL WORDS

There you have it: an introduction to accounting. I hope that this volume was able to give you a foundational education into the process of business accounting. There isn't enough space in one book to answer every possible question so I apologize if you have one left unanswered. Accounting is both a process in which we closely follow guidelines, either GAAP or IFRS, but there is a lot of room for variation. There is massive variation between companies that operate in vast and separate fields but even within a single industry there will be wildly different accounting needs that need to be handled.

The easiest need to understand is the need for financial reporting. No matter what field you are working in, your company must comply with the law and provide financial statements at regular intervals to stay on the right side of the law. Every single company has a need for financial accounting and it is this that we focused on the most throughout the book. This isn't the only type of accounting there is. In chapter one we looked at financial accounting and managerial accounting, our two big ones, but we also saw that there are other types of accounting such as tax accounting or forensic accounting. Another issue that we resolved was the confusion around bookkeeping and accounting. While both are important, and it makes sense for them to be linked together, they are still both different components of running a business. A lot of bookkeeping responsibilities have been taken over by accountants in the move to digital practices so it is common for accountants to need to learn the basics of bookkeeping these days.

In chapter two we looked at the basics of accounting. This chapter was used to define and explain some of the most important concepts in accounting. We looked at the accounting equation and saw it was made up of assets, liabilities, and shareholders' equity. To understand how these parts come together to fill out the accounting equation we looked at each of them up close to see what they mean, how they function, and how their importance is impossible to escape. Finally, we finished out this chapter with a look at what taxes are and what financial statements are. That wouldn't be the last time we explored financial statements though.

Before we could get back to financial statements we had to first learn about the various principles of accounting. We used chapter three for this purpose. We started by looking at five of the more important principles in the realm of accounting. These principles included concepts such as the full disclosure principle which reminds us to always fully disclose our earnings and the objectivity principle which reminds us that these statements are neutral and not meant to have our objective interpretation. These principles make for good accounting and they are important both for the Generally Accepted Accounting Principles (GAAP) and the International Financial Reporting Standards (IFRS). We saw that the GAAP is more rules-based while the IFRS is more standards-based. The GAAP is used in the USA while the rest of the world typically uses the IFRS. This chapter was closed out with a look at compliance and the eleven titles that were introduced in 2002 to make lack of compliance into more of a legal issue than it had been previously.

Chapter four saw us return to our financial statements. We started the chapter with a discussion of how to understand and best use financial statements. This included a discussion on their purpose, which is to say that they're used most frequently by investors, and this helped us to get a perspective on why they are so valuable. From there we moved into the financial statements themselves starting with the balance sheet, then the income statement, the cash flow statement, and finally the statement of retained earnings. These four financial statements are included together and generated for use outside of the company. Financial accounting is an external accounting system in this method.

In chapter five we had a discussion on bookkeeping. While bookkeeping is another discipline, it is a discipline that is being more and more wrapped into accounting every year. It would not surprise me if we saw bookkeeping as a field that shrinks dramatically going forward. In this chapter we looked at the purpose of a general ledger for keeping track of your financial transactions. How a general ledger works, how trial balance plays a role in the picture, and how we use debits, credits, and record journal entries were all covered so that you will have no problem using or reading a general ledger going forward.

Finally that brings us to chapter six where we turned our attention towards managerial accounting. This is the form of accounting that is focused on generating data and reports that managers and other higher-ups can use when deciding what steps the company should take next. This included a discussion on why budgeting is so important, as well as discussions on how to perform marginal analysis, cash flow analysis, how to forecast into the future and how financial leverage works.

Together these chapters serve to give you a rough idea of the world of accounting. There is far more to it than what we've been able to cover today but our goal was never to become masters. I don't want to trick you into thinking that you're some kind of super accountant now. You're far from it. But you now have enough knowledge to generate, read, and analyze financial reports and ensure that your company's accounting never strays onto the wrong side of the law. If this book has given you any help in understanding your company then I will consider my job well done.

Don't forget that the learning doesn't have to stop here. There are lots of resources available for you to continue learning about and leveling up your accounting skills. For example, we've hardly even begun to touch on investment accounting or tax accounting. Now that you have the basics, you're better equipped to seeked out and understand whatever accounting questions you have next. Don't ever stop learning, it's the best way to continue improving your business.